Book of Risks

by Susan A. Skolnick

©**National Press, Inc.**   1985
7508 Wisconsin Avenue
Bethesda, Maryland 20814

Dedication

This book is dedicated to my grandparents, Robert and Heloise Hatcher, and Sam and Flo Skolnick.

Acknowledgments

The author wishes to thank Bebe Smith, Norman Posel, June Fletcher and Brian Jenny for their contributions to the book. Special appreciation to Joel D. Joseph for writing the Business and Transportation chapters.

Cover design by Joel D. Joseph

Charts by Nancy Sanford

Library of Congress Cataloging in Publication Data

Skolnick, Susan A., 1962-
   Book of Risks

Includes index.
1. Life skills—United States. 2. Risk management—United States.
3. Social problems. I. title.
HQ 2039.U6S56   1985   658   85-9003
ISBN 0-915765-15-2
ISBN 0-915765-02-0 (pbk.)

About the Author

Susan Skolnick is a graduate of Vassar College, and has been taking risks for 23 years.

Contents

Introduction

Everyday we take risks. Many times we have no idea that we are even taking a risk. You get up, drink a cup of coffee, fish a piece of toast from the toaster with a fork, tie on your old sneakers and jog around the block. At work you buzz around the office in air-conditioned ease. After work you change clothes, leave a note on the front door for your spouse and go to the store for some steaks to barbecue. How many risks have you taken? Coffee has been linked to a variety of ailments from headaches to cancer. Your manuever with the toaster could have easily toasted you. Jogging in worn-out shoes can lead to softening of the cartilege in your knees. Your office air-conditioning may be cooling you with hazardous chemicals. The note you left on the door could have tipped off a burglar. And even if it didn't, the steaks you bought could be full of antibiotics, and charcoal grilling may introduce carcinogens into meat.

The above list may seem to imply that a person would have to tiptoe around in a sterilized spacesuit to get through the day safely. Actually, we are constantly making choices about the risks we face. We tend to discount the risks of voluntary or familiar activities and are more fearful of risks we feel imposed upon us. We are much more likely to worry about a crash when we board a plane than when we get into our car, even though we have a 30 times greater risk of dying in a car accident.

In the broadest terms, our risk of dying is influenced by factors beyond our control, including age, sex, race, and so forth. The average life expectancy in the United States is about 74.6 years, 70.4 years for men and about 77.9 years for women. White women can expect the longest lives, at 78.5 years, followed by black women at 73 years. Black and white men exhibit a large gap in expected lifespan: white men can look forward to about 71.1 years, compared with 64.4 years for black men. Your nationality may also affect your length of life: Japan, Norway, Sweden, the Netherlands and Iceland all have life expectancies of either

76 or 77 years, while lifespans in Ethiopia, Chad, Afghanistan and Nepal hover around 40 years. Knowing the risks unique to your race, sex and age group can improve your chances for a longer life. For example, the homicide rate for black Americans is six times that of their white counterparts. Blacks who are aware of this can take steps to reduce the risk of being crime victims.

The *Book of Risks* looks at risks common to most people, including personal habits, transportation, sex, and sports, and offers ways to reduce those risks. The book is not meant to alarm, or make you feel that everything is hopelessly risky, but to sensitize you to possible dangers so you can make intelligent choices.

The following chart compares the risks of various life events.

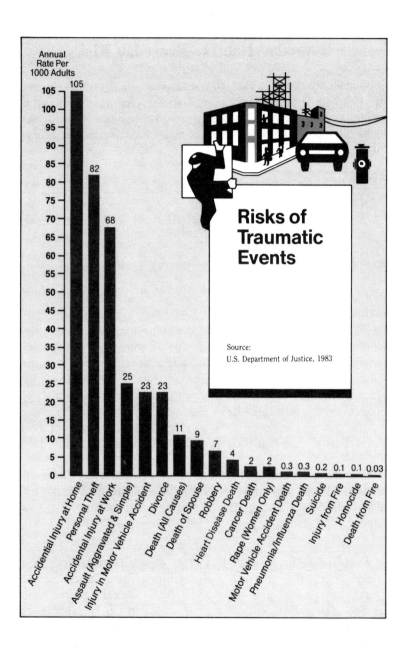

Annual Rate Per 1000 Adults

Risks of Traumatic Events

Source:
U.S. Department of Justice, 1983

Category	Rate
Accidental Injury at Home	105
Personal Theft	82
Accidental Injury at Work	68
Assault (Aggravated & Simple)	25
Injury in Motor Vehicle Accident	23
Divorce	23
Death (All Causes)	11
Death of Spouse	9
Robbery	7
Heart Disease Death	4
Cancer Death	2
Rape (Women Only)	2
Motor Vehicle Accident Death	0.3
Pneumonia/Influenza Death	0.3
Suicide	0.2
Injury from Fire	0.1
Homocide	0.1
Death from Fire	0.03

7

Chapter One
Everyday Habits, Everyday Risks

What we may be least likely to question—our daily habits—may be most likely to jeopardize our health. The other side of avoiding risks is making positive, healthful choices to preserve our health. This chapter looks at the profound effects that diet, stress, smoking and drugs have on our well-being.

Diet

Diets promising everything from weight loss, to stress reduction, to increased sex appeal regularly appear in best-selling books and supermarket tabloids. For most of us, a "diet" is something you "go on" temporarily before settling back (usually with relief) into old eating habits. The problem with most habits is that they are so deeply ingrained in our behavior that we assume they are right and natural. Most of us eat the way we do because we like to eat that way. But when people actually give up their colas and onion rings and adopt more healthful eating habits, they find their taste for the once beloved junk food diminishes.

Although scientists still dispute the degree to which diet affects our chance of illness, most agree on a set of simple guidelines which many of us would do well to adopt. Our diets are lifelong, not temporary, and, hopefully, life-giving.

Fat

An ingredient maligned by doctors and dieters, fat makes ice cream creamy, nuts nutty and many other "yummy" foods fattening. The average American obtains 40 percent of his or her daily calories from fat. Specialists recommend cutting this amount in half. Fat is necessary for good health, and should not be completely eliminated from the diet, but eating too much fat only invites trouble. Researchers have repeatedly linked high fat diets with a variety of health problems, particularly cancers of the colon, prostate, uterus and breast.

Some of the evidence:

■ Women in Japan have about one-sixth the incidence of breast cancer of American women. The Japanese diet is traditionally low in fat. Japanese women who have grown up in the U.S. have the same rate of breast cancer as American women.

■ An international study of 40 countries revealed that the breast cancer rates were highest in the countries which consumed the most dietary fat. The Netherlands had the highest death rate from breast cancer and the fattiest diet. British, Canadian, Danish, and American women also have high breast cancer rates, while women in Thailand, Japan, and the Phillipines, where diets are low in fat, have particularly low breast cancer rates.[1]

■ The incidence of breast cancer fell dramatically among British women during World War II, when wartime shortages forced women to eat less meat and dairy products, and more vegetables. After the war, women resumed their old eating habits, and the breast cancer rates went back up.

How much fat?

The average American eats six to eight times as much fat as necessary. A single tablespoon of polyunsaturated oil would fill our daily nutritional need for fat. Polyunsaturated fat is of a vegetable origin (soy, corn, safflower oils, for example), and helps *reduce* blood cholesterol when it replaces saturated fat in the diet. Saturated fat, the "bad" fat, is found in meat, whole milk, cream, and butter products, coconut and palm oil. Nutritionists recommend reducing your total intake of fat, and choosing polyunsaturated fats over saturated fats.

Reducing the amount of fat you eat requires more than spreading your butter with a lighter hand. Hidden fat lurks in marbled meat, sauces, soups, cheese, fried foods, ice cream, salad dressings, croissants, chocolate, luncheon meats, cakes, cookies and other prepared foods. Eat these foods in moderation, if at all. Choose low-fat dairy products and lean cuts of meat. Substitute fish and chicken for red meat. Remove the skin from poultry before eating.

Buy tuna packed in water rather than oil. Learn to season foods creatively so you won't feel tempted to put a pat of butter on everything. If you like sweets, angel food cake, gingersnaps, and vanilla wafers contain less fat than ice cream, chocolate or cupcakes.

When you eat out, avoid anything creamed, sauteed, fried, "crispy," au gratin, escalloped, or buttered. Choose dishes which are steamed, poached, roasted, or "cooked in its own juice." Order salad dressing on the side.

Fiber and the Lack Thereof

Seeds, the skins of fruits and vegetables, and the coatings of grains that make whole wheat whole and brown rice brown are all sources of dietary fiber. Fiber, undigested by the stomach, helps move food through the digestive system more quickly. The typical Western diet, with its plethora of convenience foods, is sadly low in fiber. To jolt our sluggish digestive systems clogged with low fiber meat, white bread, white rice and white noodles, we may swallow laxatives, which can cause permanent damage to the bowel, instead of making some intelligent changes in our diets.

A study of an African tribe in which colon cancer is practically unknown found that the people regularly eat high fiber fruits, vegetables and grains. Colon cancer is quite common in the modern western world, and scientists speculate that food more rapidly eliminated from the digestive tract means less time for cancer-causing toxins to enter the body.

Women with chronic constipation (one or two bowel movements a week), a condition rarely experienced by people eating high-fiber diets, are more likely to develop breast disease, according to a study at the University of California at San Francisco.

Salt

Sampling a spoonful of soup or a bite of casserole, we are more likely to say, "needs more salt," than "needs more basil." Our tastebuds are tuned to salt because we're so used to tasting it rather than because of nutritional need.

Most people eat much more salt than the body requires. The average American consumes two to five teaspoons of salt a day. And even if you never touch a salt shaker, you may be consuming more salt than you realize, as it is "hidden" in many prepared foods, and is the leading food additive after sugar. Besides "salty" items such as pickles, canned meats and soy sauce, salt is contained in most breads, cereals, cheese, fish, pudding and cake mixes. Salt is added to many dessert items, including some ice creams, to enhance the sweetness.

Too much salt in the diet can:

- cause high blood pressure;
- lead to fluid retention, which swells body tissues and worsens pre-menstrual tension;
- aggravate migraine headaches.

Athletes and other vigorous exercisers *do not* need extra salt; salt tablets after exertion can be dangerous.

Nutritionists recommend 1,100 to 3,300 milligrams of sodium a day. (One teaspoon contains about 2,000 milligrams.) To cut down on salt:

■ Read labels on supermarket foods, which list ingredients in order of amount contained in the product, and choose low-salt items.

■ Experiment with other seasonings, realizing that if you are used to salted dishes, foods may taste bland at first. Tell yourself you'll experiment for at least a few weeks, and make an effort to taste the subtle flavor differences in fresh vegetables whole grains, and other low-salt foods.

■ Use oil and vinegar on salads, which contains much less sodium than prepared salad dressings.

■ If you have canned meats or vegetables packed in salt water, you can remove a substantial amount of the salt by rinsing the food with water.

■ A glass of your own tap water may contain more sodium than 20 potato chips, almost 40 percent of your recommended daily amount of sodium! Many cities soften their "hard" water with sodium compounds, and salt on winter roads may contaminate the water supply. Contact your local water company to find out how much sodium is in your water.

■ Many antacids contain a lot of sodium. If you must use this product, choose the equally effective low-sodium brands.

Sugar

Some of our worst dietary habits seem to come from our desire for a limited number of tastes. We like our potatoes fried, our soups salted, and, though we may not even realize it, almost everything sweetened. The average American consumes one-third of a pound of sugar a day. If that seems higher than your daily spoonful in the coffee, note that 70 percent of the sugar in America is "hidden" in processed foods. Ketchups, soups, sauces, salad dressings, peanut butter, cake mixes and many, many other supermarket items sugar or corn syrup. And despite their down-home packaging, "all-natural" cereals and granola bars which contain brown sugar or honey instead of white sugar are rarely a better nutritional bargain. By eating a lot of sweetened products, we come to expect that sweet taste and instead of tasting the unique flavor of unsweetened food, we find it bland. A similar "taste tunnelling" occurs when we are used to eating salted foods.

The body has no need for refined sugar. Sugar gets its bad name because:

■ Excess sugar throws off the body's internal balance of glucose and insulin so that the blood sugar level actually drops for a period, which can cause fatigue and irritability.

■ Because sugar's calories are concentrated, you often don't feel full until you've already eaten too much, leading to weight gain. Think of times you've found room to eat a sweet dessert even though you were too full to eat another bite of dinner.

■ Sugar's empty calories may take the place of more nutritious foods, resulting in deficiencies.

■ Too much sugar may lead to diabetes, especially in people with a genetic predisposition to the disease.

■ Researchers have found that nations where more refined sugar is eaten have higher breast cancer mortality rates.[2]

■ Unless you rinse and brush right after eating a sweet, you risk tooth decay.

Slimming Down Your Risks

Thirty-four million Americans are obese—20 percent over their desirable weight—according to a recent National Institute of Health panel on Obesity. Serious health problems can accompany those extra pounds. Studies have clearly linked obesity with cancer, particularly cancers of the colon, rectum, and prostate in men, and cancers of the gall bladder, breast, cervix, ovaries and uterus in women.

■ Even as little as 10 extra pounds can intensify arthritis pain and stiffness in the joints.

■ Extra weight can increase blood pressure and the risk of heart attack.

■ Extra weight can make surgery difficult, as fat tissue bleeds more.

■ A study of children's performance in math and reading revealed that the overweight students had the highest incidence of under-achievement. Overweight children often eat too many foods which are high in calories but low in nutrition, and this malnutrition is associated with learning problems.

The following factors put you at a greater risk if you are already overweight, according to Dr. Ethan Sims of the University of Vermont:

■ A close relative has had diabetes, heart attack or stroke before age 60.

■ Your mother has had a baby weighing more than 9 pounds.

■ You have had a baby weighing more than 9 pounds.

■ You have gained more than 25 pounds since you were 20.

■ You smoke more than half a pack of cigarettes a day.

■ You suffered diabetes during pregnancy.

■ You have high blood pressure.

■ Your abdomen is wider than your hips.

■ You can pinch more than two inches of fat just above your abdomen.

How You Should Modify Your Diet

The American Cancer Society and the National Academy of Sciences have both issued guidelines for a wholesome diet most likely to decrease your chances of disease. Their basic suggestions follow:

■ Cut down on fat.

■ Eat more high-fiber foods, such as whole grains,cereals, fresh fruits and vegetables.

■ Eat foods rich in vitamin A and C. Fruits and vegetables which may have a particularly protective effect include cantaloupes, watermelons, apricots, peaches, strawberries, citrus fruits, parsley, peppers, cabbage, broccoli, brussels sprouts, cauliflower, squash and carrots.

■ Avoid too many smoked foods and foods cured with salt and nitrites. Salt-cured and pickled foods may increase the risk of stomach and esophagus cancer.

■ Eat a wide variety of foods. If you eat the same foods most of the time, your diet may lack essential nutrients.

■ Avoid eating the burnt parts of food. Charcoal grilling may produce carcinogens.

■ Avoid drinking extremely hot water, coffee or tea. Research in Japan suggests that these practices may contribute to stomach cancer.

■ Drink alcoholic beverages only in moderation. Heavy drinkers, especially those who smoke, substantially increase their risk of developing cancers of the larynx, oral cavity and esophagus.

Stress

Altering your response to stress may be the most significant step you can take to preserve your physical and mental well-being. It can also be a truly challenging task.

In a landmark study on stress, Dr. Meyer Friedman and Dr. Ray Rosenman divided the population into Type A's and Type B's. People with Type A personalities lead rushed lives, feel driven to achieve and try to do as much as possible in as little time as possible. Type A's are generally more aggressive, impatient and hostile than the more relaxed Type B's. Of course, slicing the entire population into two groups neglects the countless variations in people's personalities, but it has indeed been established that the more stress in a person's life, the greater the risk of illness. Friedman's study found that Type A's have about twice the risk of heart attack of Type B's.

Besides the more serious consequences of heart disease and high blood pressure, a whole catalogue of annoying symptoms may flare up because of stress. Rashes, stiff or aching muscles, headaches, acne, reduced resistence to colds and flu, insomnia, indigestion, and even conditions such as hemorrhoids can be brought on by stress.

How To Calm Down

Reducing stress in your life requires a shift of attitude. You may be afraid to stop driving yourself because you worry that you will get nothing done, you will get sloppy, you will lose control. But if you look closely, you may see that your reaction to stress is actually working against your ability to create and contribute. Can you really think clearly if you are fuming in a traffic jam? Type A's often get frustrated and angry when they feel others are impeding their progress, but in most cases, aggressively expressing anger just alienatesand angers others. Type A's who learn to modify their behavior by slowing down and practicing patience usually discover that they are still productive, and a whole lot happier. The following is a list of suggestions for dealing with stress.

■ Deeply consider what is truly important to you, and ask yourself whether your current preoccupations help or hinder your attaining your goals.

■ Become aware of how you "talk" to yourself in your mind. Most of us constantly monitor and judge our behavior. If your self-talks are unnecessarily negative, they're doing more harm than good. If you concentrate on your good qualities and make an effort to develop them, you'll have less to criticize yourself about.

■ Once you've eased up on yourself a bit, you'll find it easier to see the good qualities in others as well, making yourself less prone to irritability and hostility.

■ Make a point of relaxing, especially in situations which usually make you impatient. Use waits in lines and traffic jams as opportunities to observe what stress does to you and how you can relax by breathing slowly and quieting your mind.

■ Try not to live by numbers. Dr. Friedman notes that "Type A's tend to be over-numerical. They have to learn to stop thinking in terms of how much, how many, how fast, what's the cost, what's the yield."

■ Exercise regularly, at least three times a week for 20 minutes. See your doctor first, and start gradually. Whatever you do, don't set yourself up for injury by throwing yourself into exercise with Type A urgency!

■ Become aware of your dietary habits and make a point of eating a wholesome breakfast, limiting your consumption of fatty, salty and sugary foods.

■ Using nicotine, alcohol, caffeine and drugs are all dangerous, as well as futile, ways to control our experience. Quitting smoking is probably the most valuable thing you can do for your health. Limit alcohol intake to two drinks a day at the very most, preferably much less than that. Too much caffeine can make you nervous and unable to relax. Become aware of the situations which make you desire that cigarette, cocktail, or cup of coffee and ask yourself whether you want such desires to control you.

Smoking and Drinking

People may know more about the risks of smoking and drinking than any other two activities which they persist in doing. An incredible 30 percent of all people in the U.S. die prematurely each year because of alcohol and tobacco use.

Alcohol

Although many may believe that nearly everyone drinks alcohol, 40 percent of Americans are non-drinkers. Half of the alcohol consumed in the U.S. each year is drunk by one-tenth of the population. About 60 percent of Americans over age 18 are regular drinkers. More men are heavy drinkers than women (14 percent of American men are heavy drinkers, compared with four percent of American women.) Hispanics have higher heavy drinking rates than other groups in the U.S.

Alcohol use is associated with one-third of all traffic accidents, and a substantial number of industrial accidents, drownings, burns, and falls, as well as many cases of rape, child abuse and family violence in general. According to a report released by the Department of Health and Human Services:

 ■ Alcoholics die ten times more often in fires than non-alcoholics.

 ■ Alcoholics commit suicide six to 15 times more often than non-alcoholics.

 ■ Pregnant women who drink risk having a child with low infant birth weight, and reduced intelligence or motor development. An average of two drinks a day can lead to miscarriage.

 ■ More than half of all cases of family violence are estimated to be associated with alcohol.

 ■ Cancer of the mouth, tongue, pharynx and esophagus are more common in alcoholics than in non-alcoholics.

 ■ Alcohol can precipitate a gout attack.

 ■ Male sexual performance and functioning are significantly

15

altered by alcohol consumption. Seventy to 80 percent of alcoholics suffer from impotence or reduced sexual drive.

■ Alcohol use can cause high blood pressure. One study found that when men aged 50 to 74 increased their alcohol consumption from one to three drinks a day, their blood pressure went up the same amount it would have if they had gone from 165 to 195 pounds.

Most people know that alcoholism is dangerous, but what are the risks of "social drinking?" Some recent studies suggest that moderate drinkers live longer than non-drinkers. A drink or two a day could actually benefit the heart, according to these studies, by raising the level of blood proteins which protect against heart disease. If you are going to drink, eat something about fifteen minutes beforehand, and drink slowly in a relaxed setting. Alcohol tends to exaggerate whatever mood you are in.

On the other hand, drunk drivers who are "social drinkers" are just as dangerous as drunk drivers who are alcoholics. Any alcohol in the brain means you have reduced motor control and thus a greater risk of having an accident. Alcohol is caloric, so social drinking can make you overweight. Too much alcohol can also damage your skin tone.

Smoking

Most of us know smoking is dangerous. How could inhaling smoke, the gas of burning material in which particles of soot are suspended, *not* be dangerous? Smoking causes half a million deaths a year, according to the U.S. Department of Agriculture: 147,000 cancer deaths, 240,000 heart disease deaths, 61,000 deaths from respiratory diseases, 4,000 deaths from injuries—such as fires—and 15,000 other deaths. About 4,000 infants die as a result of their mothers' smoking.[3]

■ The average smoker loses one day in five from work and one day in ten in bed because of illness.[4]

■ Women who smoke may have an earlier menopause.[5]

■ Smoking while pregnant reduces the oxygen available to the fetus, and raises the risk of miscarriage, low birth weight, and delivering a stillborn. The children of women who smoked during pregnancy have twice the risk of developing pneumonia and bronchitis than children of non-smokers.

Cigarette smoke can harm non-smokers, too. A study in Japan found that non-smoking wives of smokers were four times more likely to develop lung cancer than women whose husbands did not smoke. After 30 minutes in a smoke-filled room, a non-smoker's heart beats faster, his blood pressure goes up, and the level of carbon monoxide in his blood increases.

The "Harmless" Drugs: Caffeine and Aspirin

A Mellow Brew?

Caffeine: it clears the head, quickens reaction time, and sharpens sensory perceptions. One cup of coffee allows typists to type faster and make fewer mistakes. Unfortunately, caffeine's few benefits are overwhelmingly cancelled by its negative side effects. Caffeine is a habit-forming drug widely available to children as well as adults. Caffeine has been linked to a battery of medical problems: heart disease, cancer, gastrointestinal ailments, kidney disease, low blood sugar, fetal damage and hyperactivity, not to mention nervousness, anxiety, mental depression and fatigue. The extent of caffeine's harmful effects has been disputed by some researchers, although most would agree that consuming too much caffeine is indeed dangerous.

Americans drink 450 million cups of coffee a day, which is actually less than they drank in 1966, when 95 percent of those between 30 and 59 drank coffee, according to the National Coffee Association. The Swiss, Danes, Norwegians, Swedes, Belgians, Dutch and French drink even more than Americans. Americans drink four times more coffee than tea, while the English, Scotch, Welsh and Irish drink nine cups of tea for every cup of coffee. Tea usually contains less caffeine than coffee, depending on how strong the brew.

Significant amounts of caffeine are also contained in soft drinks, cocoa and chocolate products, and in some over-the- counter drugs such as aspirin, stimulant drugs such as Vivarin, menstrual-discomfort

17

drugs, weight loss drugs and cold and allergy medications. Caffeine has some definitely nasty effects:

- The Center for Science in the Public Interest concluded after reviewing the relevant scientific studies that caffeine consumption by pregnant women increases the risk of birth defects and other reproductive problems.

- Sceptics abound, but cancer of the pancreas, stomach and bladder have all been linked to coffee consumption.

- A recent Stanford University study found that both sedentary and moderately active men aged 30 to 55 who drink more than two or three cups of coffee a day may increase their risk of heart disease.

Children are particularly sensitive to caffeine, and unfortunately, many young people consume a lot of it (the average teenage boy downs three bottles of soda pop a day). Not only can caffeine cause the restlessness, nervousness, nausea and insomnia experienced by adults, but it is also associated with affecting learning ability and contributing to hyperactivity. Cola can also lead to ulcers and trigger asthma in children.

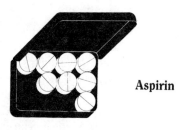

Aspirin

You can buy it from vending machines, gas stations and gift shops. It's kept in purses, desk drawers and kitchen cabinets. In a survey of American youth, one in four college students had used aspirin in the previous 48 hours, and about 40 percent of 4th to 12th graders surveyed had taken it during the past week. Aspirin is so widely used, many people don't even consider it a drug. Americans take over 20 billion aspirin tablets every year; the country consumes over 20 tons a day.

But aspirin is not harmless. Of all over-the-counter drugs, aspirin causes the most adverse reactions and is a major cause of childhood poisoning. What is aspirin good for? Arthritis is often treated effectively with aspirin, which can reduce inflammation in the joints and delay and lessen crippling. Aspirin is also generally effective for muscular aches and pains of moderate severity, but should only be used for a short period without consulting a doctor. Do not rely on aspirin for recurring or chronic pain, especially if you have recurring headaches—see a doctor.

Aspirin can also reduce fevers, but more and more specialists advise against immediately trying to lower your temperature when you are ill. Fever is the body's natural reaction to infection; white blood cells can fight infection more effectively and the body can make more antibodies when the temperature is higher. Most doctors believe that temperatures of 102 and below do not require treatment.

Children with the flu or chicken pox should *not* be given aspirin, as it has been linked with Reye's syndrome, a disease characterized by sudden vomiting and fever. It is fatal in 20 to 30 percent of the cases. No link between Reye's syndrome and aspirin substitutes have been found.

Aspirin can truly wreak havoc on your stomach and intestines. Heartburn, dyspepsia, stomach discomfort, nausea and vomiting are some of the more *minor* effects of aspirin. Stomach ulcers, erosion of and bleeding from the lining of the stomach, and even gastrointestinal hemorrhage are more serious side effects which usually occur when people take high doses, but can also effect hypersensitive individuals.

Buffered aspirins do not necessarily protect the stomach from damage. Enteric coatings on aspirin, however, delay absorption of aspirin until it reaches the intestine, making ulcers and stomach erosion less likely. People who already have ulcers should not take aspirin.

Other people who should avoid aspirin, unless otherwise advised by a physician:

- Patients expecting surgery, people taking blood-thinning drugs and those with liver disease. Aspirin's tendency to prolong bleeding can complicate these conditions.

- People with gout. Aspirin can reduce the elimination of uric acid by the kidneys, thereby worsening gout.

- Diabetics. Aspirin interferes with some drugs used to control diabetes.

- Pregnant women, especially in the last three months of pregnancy. Infants of aspirin users have significantly lower birth weights and are more likely to die around the time of birth. Prenatal aspirin use has also been associated with newborn hypertension and increased hemorrhaging in both mothers and newborns. Prolonged pregnancies, length of labor and difficulties in delivery have also been linked with aspirin use. Although studies are not definitely conclusive, a study in Finland found that mothers who had infants with cleft lip and/or cleft palate had taken aspirin during their pregnancies three times as often as mothers with normal children.

Marijuana

Few marijuana smokers will vow to quit their habit after reading a list of marijuana's unhealthy effects. That is quite unfortunate, because this drug, for too long considered a harmless, "soft" drug, causes some very un-gentle damage to the smoker's physical and emotional well-being.

Marijuana contains more tar and more cancer-causing substances than tobacco smoke. The THC in marijuana is toxic to the lungs and other internal organs. More than 80 percent of marijuana smokers are also cigarette smokers, thus multiplying their risk of lung disease.

- Marijuana smoke damages anti-infection white blood cells in the lungs.
- Most marijuana contains a common soil fungus which can lead to serious lung disease.[6]
- Men who smoke marijuana risk lowering their testosterone levels, reducing sperm production, and triggering the production of abnormal sperm.
- Women smokers increase their risk of suffering from menstrual irregularities. Pregnant women who smoke marijuana may risk more miscarriages or have infants with lowered birth weights.
- People under the influence of marijuana have impaired motor coordination and visual ability, and are less capable of making clear decisions. "Stoned" drivers are a hazard on the road.
- Marijuana and its by-products can remain in the body for months after use, with unknown damaging effects.

Cocaine

Cocaine use has increased dramatically in the past ten years in the U.S., Europe, and the more developed nations of Asia and Latin America. Cocaine is considered a "sophisticated" drug, the delightfully naughty vice of the rock star and young executive. Its high price, however, has not prevented teenagers from sampling or becoming hooked on the drug. The National Institute of Drug Abuse found that about 16 percent of high school seniors had used cocaine at some time.

In 1982, the Institute found that at least 21.6 million Americans had tried cocaine, that 12 million had used it in the year preceding the survey, and that 4.2 million were regular users of the drug. These figures are undoubtedly conservative, as the survey did not include college students, military personnel, or anyone under 18 years old.

Based on a survey by the toll-free hotline 800-COCAINE, about two-thirds of cocaine users are male. Most are white and educated. Many use other drugs such as alcohol and narcotics to ease the depression or "crash" which follows a cocaine high. Most users will continue to do cocaine regardless of its damaging effects on their health, work, and relationships.

In the body, cocaine constricts blood vessels, raises blood pressure and makes the heart beat faster. Mucous membranes dry out and crack and bleed. Little crystals of cocaine can erode the cartilage separating the nostrils.

Cocaine users often start as occasional, "recreational" users, and then become hooked. Their addiction typically leads to numerous unfortunate consequences as the user becomes more obsessed with the drug. Relationships and careers fall apart. Users may sniff (or shoot up) their entire savings, and turn to stealing to support their habit. Psychologically, the user is commonly afflicted with depression, anxiety, irritability, difficulty concentrating, loss of interest in work or other activities, and paranoia. When cocaine abuse gets bad, it often gets very bad. Just like the laboratory monkeys who choose cocaine over food and drink until they die, the coke addict may stop eating, sleeping, washing, and talking to people, doing cocaine continually until his supply runs out.

Cocaine abusers can get help from the 24-hour-a-day hotline, 800-COCAINE, or they can join a support group like Cocaine Anonymous or seek private professional help.

Regular cocaine use can cause chronic insomnia and fatigue, nasal problems, severe headaches, seizures, loss of consciousness, nausea, vomiting and decreased sexual performance. Cocaine can also damage the vocal cords, a concern for more than one rock star who indulges in the drug. Regular use can affect vision and cause vitamin deficiencies.

Notes
1. "Nutrition, Hormones, and Cancer," *Medical Times,* May 1983
2. *New Scientist,* March 10, 1983
3. *Population and Development Review,* R.T. Ravenholt
4. Maryland State Medical Association
5. *Acta Medica Scandinavica,* vol. 212, no. 3, 1982
6. *Getting Tough on Gateway Drugs,* Robert L. DuPont, Jr., M.D., American Psychiatric Press

Chapter Two
Homegrown Hazards

The National Safety Council reports that about 20,000 people die in household accidents each year. In addition, 23.5 million people, one in ten Americans, are injured in home accidents. Five and a half million accidents are severe enough to require that the victim be confined to bed.

 Keep It Edible

Improper handling of food in the home causes nearly two million cases of food poisoning each year. You are in danger of poisoning yourself if you:

■ eat prepared foods which have been at room temperature for over two hours, especially starchy foods, cooked and cured meats, cheese and meat salads.

■ eat canned food with any of the following signs: milky liquid surrounding the vegetables, badly dented cans, loose lids, or swollen cans or lids. These signs indicate a rare but deadly food poisoning, botulism. Don't even *taste* a canned good if you suspect botulism.

■ eat undercooked meat, pork, or poultry. If you own a microwave, you must make sure food cooks thoroughly. See suggestions below.

The basic rule for avoiding food poisoning: **keep food hot or cold, and clean.**

■ Cook meat thoroughly, and check for doneness with a meat thermometer. Since microwaving may leave some areas of food undercooked, be sure to rotate food in the oven and then let stand outside the oven for the prescribed amount of time.

- The more you handle food, the greater the chance of contamination. Don't rewrap store-wrapped goods unless the wrapping is torn.
- It's a common practice, but avoid thawing meat on the kitchen counter. Room temperature is ideal for bacterial growth. Instead, put frozen meat in the refrigerator to thaw overnight.
- Another common practice is to let leftovers cool on the counter before refrigerating, but it's safest to put them straight into the refrigerator. You can put plastic and pyrex containers directly into the refrigerator without danger of cracking.
- Don't store fresh meat in the fridge for more than one to two days. Always pay attention to "Sell By" and "Use By" dates on supermarket products.
- Wash your hands thoroughly before food preparation.
- Bacteria can harbor in dirty sponges or dishtowels. Keep yours clean. Bits of food stuck to cookware can also become breeding grounds for bacteria. An outbreak of food poisoning at a summer camp was traced to a single pot with particles of food stuck to the side.
- If any dish or utensil comes in contact with raw meat, wash that item before using it for the cooked food. Chefs for one wedding party did not follow this precaution, with sorry consequences. Cooked turkey was sliced on the same board the raw turkeys had sat on earlier, recontaminating the cooked turkey with bacteria that had been killed by the high cooking temperatures. The cooked turkey then sat out at room temperature for a few hours before the reception, where they were reheated in a steam heater. Nearly 80 percent of the guests became violently ill.
- If you stuff a turkey or chicken, remember that any bacteria in raw poultry can get into the stuffing, so to avoid contamination:
    1. Don't stuff the bird until you're ready to cook it.
    2. Check the stuffing with a meat thermometer—it should reach 165 degrees Farenheit.
    3. Separate stuffing from the bird before serving.[1]

Pharmaceutical Steak, Chinese Restaurant Syndrome and Other Avoidables

- Acid foods, such as apples or tomatoes, cooked in copper pots may dissolve the copper, leading to copper poisoning.
- About 80 percent of swine, 60 percent of cattle, and 30 percent of chickens in the U.S. are fed antibiotic-laced feed to encourage growth. Scientists believe that ingesting such meat can lead to a reduced effectiveness of antibiotics prescribed by a doctor. You might have to do some shopping, but it is possible to purchase organic meats uncontaminated with antibiotics or other pharmaceuticals.

■ Don't interrupt cooking—bacteria can easily grow in partially cooked food.

■ Always reheat leftovers thoroughly.

■ If you eat home-canned foods, always boil contents a full ten minutes before serving.

■ Though you may consider Japanese sushi (raw fish) a delicacy, there is nothing delicate about the nausea, diarrhea, abdominal cramps or constipation that could follow the ingestion of fish infected with an intestinal parasite. In some instances, anemia and even death have occurred. Doctors in Japan treated 178 patients with a roundworm infection over a 15 year period. The parasite is quite rare in the U.S., where only 21 cases have been reported since 1972, most of which were not very serious.

■ MSG (monosodium glutamate) in Chinese food (and other foods from the supermarket—check labels) can cause "Chinese Restaurant Syndrome." Some people are more sensitive than others, but many notice themselves experiencing headaches, burning sensations, chest pain and/or fatigue after eating in a Chinese restaurant. Ask the waiter to hold the MSG. Eating some non-MSG food before the meal can slow absorption of MSG.

 Poisoning

A more extensive review of the risks of poisoning appears in the Chapter Eight. Many people associate accidental poisoning with children, and while about three times as many children as adults are poisoned each year, the number of poisoning *deaths* for each group is very close. Adults should take precautions against poisoning themselves as well as their children.

Always follow directions for taking medications. Never transfer medicine from its original container to another. This practice can only invite confusion. Never take medicine in the dark. Do not keep medicine after the illness for which it was prescribed has ended.

Open a window when cleaning. Avoid spraying pesticides on windy days, and always spray downwind. Aerosol products pose a triple danger: the cans may explode if punctured or overheated; you may spray the contents of a can in your eyes, or inhale the toxic fumes. Heavy use of aerosols has been linked with lung cancer and is also known to damage the enviroi ment. So many alternatives exist, such as pump sprays, or products in liquid or solid form, that it is easy to avoid aerosol use all together.

Falls

Nearly 20,000 people die each year of injuries from falls. The National Safety Council's committee on fall prevention estimates that, counting medical care bills, days lost from work and lawsuits, falls cost about $1 million *an hour* in the U.S. Three-quarters of these people are aged 65 or over. Fatal falls from windows often involve small children who lean against loose screens. Males fall more often than females, especially from ladders and scaffolds. Check your home for the following hazard sites:

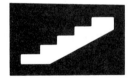

Stairs

About 350,000 serious accidents occur on stairs each year. Make your stairs safe with adequate lighting, non-skid stair surfaces, and sturdy handrails on both sides. Use extra care when carrying packages up the stairs, or when wearing high heels, long dresses or stockinged feet.

Use gates at the top and bottom of all staircases if toddlers live in your home. Choose gates with a tight mesh surface: children have gotten their heads stuck in the collapsible wooden gates with the diamond openings, and some have even been strangled to death.

Kitchen & Bath

Invest in a sturdy step stool to reach things in your kitchen; don't climb on chairs or countertops. And though you may want to keep goodies such as cookies and chips out of your child's easy reach, it's best not to store them in high places or above the stove, where ambitious children could fall if they try to maneuver their way into the cabinet.

In the bathroom, attach a non-slip mat or non-skid strips securely to the tub floor. Use a non-skid mat on the floor beside the tub to avoid the risk of slipping when getting out of the shower. If elderly people live in the home, grab rails next to the tub and toilet can prevent falls.

Other Tips

■ Use plug-in night lights in the hall and near your bed.

■ Secure any windows which children can reach. Locks are available which allow windows to be opened only a few inches for ventilation.

■ A recent study of elderly victims of falls suggests that in nearly half of the accidents, the person had been taking a medication such as a diuretic or sedative/hypnotic which caused dizziness, confusion or unsteadiness.

Outdoors

Each year, 300-400 people die from ladder falls, and another 40,000 suffer disabling injuries. You can avoid disaster by investing in a high quality ladder approved by the American Ladder Institute (yes, such an organization exists). Do not lean your ladder too steeply against the wall—a good rule of thumb is for every four feet of height you want to reach, place the bottom of the ladder one foot away from the wall. If you are climbing to the roof, make sure the top of your ladder extends at least three feet beyond the roof edge, so you don't risk slipping while boosting yourself up over the edge.

■ Icy sidewalks can be deadly. Nearly one-half of all falls on slippery ice result in broken bones, one-third result in sprained or bruised ankles, and more than one-sixth in strained muscles. To avoid falls on the ice:

- Clear snow from sidewalks before it packs down and becomes slippery.

- Sprinkle rock salt, potassium chloride, or calcium chloride on walkways. Sand is also effective, and better for the environment.

- Wear shoes with traction-creating soles. Many rubber boots are too slippery. Metal cleats are available which strap easily onto shoes and allow you to walk on smooth ice.

- Lean forward as you walk and take small steps, keeping knees bent slightly. Hold your arms out at waist level for balance.

- Don't keep your hands in your pockets. Some people have been seriously hurt because they couldn't get their hands out in time to break a fall, and landed on their faces or heads. Use a backpack to carry your things and leave your hands free.

- Knock the snow off the bottom of shoes before entering buildings.

- Remember that you're likely to be careful after a heavy freezing rain, but many falls occur when the snow on the ground melts during the day and freezes at night, covering pavements with sheets of ice.

- Don't go outside in your slippers to retrieve the morning paper, even if it's "just a few steps." Don't be casual; use the handrail.

If you begin to fall, don't try to break the fall with your arms. To avoid breaking limbs, try to relax and roll into the fall to spread the impact over as large an area as possible.

 **Fires**

Over 600,000 fires a year take place in the U.S. Fire is the second leading cause of death in the home after falls, claiming about 4,000 lives a year. In one- and two-family dwellings, heating is the most common cause of fires, followed by cooking, deliberate setting, electrical distribution and smoking.[2] About half of all fires are caused by cigarettes, often when the smoker has been drinking alcohol. Indeed, smoking is the most common cause of fire deaths, while 35 percent of those killed in fires have blood alcohol levels above the legal level of drunkenness.[3] Of fires that cause multiple deaths, 80 percent occur at night, with the young, the elderly and the poor victimized more than other groups. A cigarette igniting upholstered furniture in a living room is the most common scenario for a multiple death fire.

Elderly adults and children often start fires. Children, despite the well known rule, still play with matches. The elderly may neglect turning off electrical appliances, and a weakened sense of smell could delay the discovery of a fire.

Improper use of electrical equipment is at fault for about 15 percent of home fires. The following suggestions could prevent disaster:

- Don't just replace a blown fuse, find out why it blew.
- Avoid overloading outlets, and running electrical cords under rugs or furniture, which can become frayed without you noticing.
- Call an electrician if you notice any unexplainable hot spots on the walls.
- Look for the UL seal on any radiant or space heaters you buy, and get one that shuts off when knocked down. Keep the heater away from flammable materials such as drapes or clothing.
- 138,000 fires were caused by smoking materials in 1975. People continue to ignore the old rule "never smoke in bed," and houses continue to go up in smoke. Also avoid smoking while relaxing on a sofa or easy chair, where you could fall asleep.
- Cooking oil causes many kitchen fires. Never douse with water. Smother flames with pot lid or baking soda or salt.
- Wear snug fitting clothing while cooking; blousy sleeves could too easily catch fire if accidently brushed across a burner. Avoid wearing nylon, which is quite flammable.
- Always turn off iron after use.
- In 1982, wood or coal stoves started 47,300 fires in the U.S., injured 5,220 people with burns, and killed 110. Always position your stove at least three feet from the walls, ceiling, furniture and drapes. The insulating pad underneath the stove should extend at least 18 inches in front of the ash removal door. Remove any obstructions, including bird nests, from the chimney and stove pipe, and clean out any buildup of creosote, which is a highly flammable by-product of burning wood. Trim any overgrown trees or vines near the chimney to reduce the risk of fire from a stray spark. And remember to keep a fire extinguisher near your stove.

Smoke Detectors

About 90 percent of all fire fatalities, and over 80 percent of the fire injuries in 1982 occurred in homes without smoke detectors. Unprotected homes also suffered 87 percent of the total residential property loss. Clearly, smoke detectors are worth the investment. Ideally, install one detector in each sleeping area, and one on each level of your home, including the basement. If you only have one detector, locate it between the bedrooms and the rest of the house, but closer to the bedrooms. Do not install the detector less than six inches from the corner, as this area gets little air circulation. To keep yours working properly, remember to gently vacuum once a year and replace the batteries.

Shattered Spoons, Exploding Soda Bottles and Other Miscellaneous Hazards

■ If your toast gets stuck in the toaster, don't risk electrocution by trying to retrieve it with a fork or knife. Unplug the toaster first, and better yet, use wooden tongs instead of a metal utensil.

■ Pushing garbage down the garbage disposal with a spoon while it's running can send splinters flying into your face. Avoid the similarly dangerous practice of stirring mixtures in a blender when it's running, and always unplug a mixer before inserting or removing the blades, even if the switch is off.

■ Remember that stove burners can be dangerously hot though not red, and inform children.

■ To avoid exploding soft-drink bottles, do not store in hot closets or shake bottles. Always point cap away when opening, as bottles may explode despite your precautions.

■ At least 600 people are electrocuted each year in their homes. Touching exposed sockets and using electrical appliances and lamps with faulty wiring can cause death. Plug plastic safety plugs into any empty sockets, especially if there are children in the house.

■ Antennas cause many home electrocutions. In a typical scenario, someone is erecting or taking down an antenna when it leans over and touches a power line. Better to let an expert install your antenna.

■ Twenty to twenty five people a year, mostly children under 5, electrocute themselves in the bathtub with electrical appliances. Hair dryers cause 60 percent of the deaths. The appliances *do not need to be turned on,* just plugged in. The water completes the circuit. Keep appliances such as hair dryers, curling irons, and radios out of the bathroom all together if possible, and never touch them when your skin is wet.

■ Children left alone in the bathtub may turn the hot water tap on and scald themselves. Set your hot water heater no higher than 120 degrees.

The Door that Wasn't There . . .

Each year, 40,000 people injure themselves by trying to walk through glass doors and windows they believe are open. 6,000 of these victims require hospitalization. To prevent this danger, and to keep birds from trying to fly through large panes of glass and breaking their necks, apply decals to glass, or cover with wall hangings.

Beware the Simple Toothpick

■ Hospital emergency rooms treat about 8,000 Americans each year for injuries caused by toothpicks. Children stick them in ears and eyes, people swallow them inadvertently. In one case, surgeons operated unsuccesfully to determine the cause of a man's intestinal abscess. They found only after his death the cause—a toothpick puncturing his gut. Dr. Lawrence Budnick, who has investigated toothpick dangers, recommends caution to partygoers who drink and munch hors d'oeuvres—alcohol can dull the senses so you don't feel the stick in your mouth, and sometimes the crab puff or whorl of paté conceals the toothpick.

Outdoor and Workshop Risks

■ Cluttered areas are dangerous areas. Keep your garage free of old newspapers, oil-soaked rags and other flammable materials. Store all chemicals out of children's reach, forbid playing there and lock the door.

■ Never, ever, store gasoline in a garage, where the smallest spark can ignite escaped vapors.

■ A recent Environmental Protection Agency study calculated that gasoline vapors from self-service pumps could cause 34 cancer deaths a year. 70 percent of gas stations in the U.S. are self-service stations. The government may someday require rubber sleeves around pump nozzles.

■ Power Saws: Power saws injure 100,000 Americans a year. Toes, hands and fingers are often lost in these accidents. This tool must always be used with extreme care, and only after reading all instructions for its use. Removal of the blade guard, and circular saw blades that throw the saw back toward user cause many accidents, according to the Consumer Product Safety Commission.

Precautions: All power equipment should bear the UL (Underwriters Laboratory) approved seal. Tools should be grounded with a three prong plug, or labeled as double insulated. Keep all flammable materials away from the equipment when using. Wear safety goggles, snug fitting clothing and protect your hearing with earplugs.

■ 50,000 people are injured each year while mowing their lawns. The mower blades cut feet and hands. Objects such as rocks and sticks are shot from the housing and hit the user, who may lose an eye or suffer lacerations. Reel mowers are generally safer than rotary mowers.

Minimize mowing hazards by wearing heavy shoes, raking the lawn before mowing and picking up any loose objects, and never pulling the mower toward you. Always shut off the mower and allow to cool before refueling. To avoid slipping, do not mow wet grass, and mow *across* slopes rather than up and down.

Always paint in a well-ventilated room. Paint sprayers, if accidently triggered, can shoot paint onto the skin, penetrate it, and damage tissues.

■ Many hobbies, such as photography, painting or furniture refinishing, can generate dangerous fumes. Others, such as woodworking or metalworking, generate dust which can damage the lungs if inhaled. Glues and chemicals can irritate the skin. Basic hobbying guidelines: read instructions on all products. Wear the appropriate goggles, gloves, and/or face masks. Work in a properly ventilated room, and clean up well. Keep all foods and beverages out of the workshops, and avoid touching hands to mouth and eyes. Screw lids on tight, and keep unsupervised children out of the workshop. Never use power tools with children in the same room.

Silence is Golden

One in 10 people have some degree of hearing loss in the U.S. Many people accept hearing loss as an inevitable effect of aging, but many cases are undoubtedly due to the environment. Simply put, the major cause of hearing disorders is excessive exposure to noise. Too much noise is also responsible for a list of sundry stress-related disorders that can lead to heart disease, low infant birth weights, insomnia, anxiety, headaches, colitis, and ulcers.

Hearing loss can occur when daily exposure averages about 70 decibels, according to researchers at the Environmental Protection Agency. A noisy restaurant, a vacuum cleaner, and the general noise level in urban neighborhoods can generate 70 decibels and above.

To protect your hearing:

■ Wear earplugs in particularly noisy places. Carry a pair of inexpensive foam plugs in your purse or briefcase.

- When you can control noise levels, such as while watching television or listening to music, limit your exposure to several brief periods rather than one long period.
- Do not blast your ears with headphone stereos. If you can feel a vibration, it's too loud.
- If you're house hunting, check out the neighborhood during the week as well as on a quiet Sunday. Try to find a quiet place to live.
- Make your home quieter by installing carpets and drapes, putting foam pads under appliances, caulking windows and installing storm windows. Plastic garbage cans are quieter than metal ones.

The Risk of Rabies from Rover

The pet owners of the 90 million dogs and cats in America can rest assured that contracting a pet-borne disease—a zoonose—is a fairly rare occurence. People catch most diseases from other people. Nevertheless, diseases can spread from pets to humans, although they usually require very close contact with the infected animal or its excretions, and can thus generally be avoided with proper hygiene and regular pet vaccinations.

On the down side, infected animals rarely exhibit noticeable symptoms. The risk of catching a disease from a pet is higher for children, who are more likely to kiss and play closely with the animal, and who often put their hands in their mouths. Their lower number of antibodies also increases their susceptibility to disease.

Rabies, Roundworms, and Salmonella

Only one or two people catch rabies in the U.S. each year, and wild animals are usually the carriers. About 30,000 people get postbite rabies shots each year as a precaution against this dangerous virus which attacks the brain and nervous system.

More common than rabies is salmonella, a bacteria which usually causes food poisoning. Dogs, frogs, aquarium snails, turtles and the feces of pet chicks can be contaminated with salmonella. After an estimated 280,000 cases of salmonella poisoning a year were traced to pet turtles, the U.S. Food and Drug Administration banned their sale.

Infected dogs can shed the bacteria in their feces, while showing no symptoms. Symptoms of salmonella poisoning are fever, vomiting, diarrhea, and possibly even death in the very young, sick or elderly. The best way to avoid infection is to wash hands after handling pets, keep away from animal droppings, and don't keep birds in rooms where food is prepared or eaten.

Roundworms is one of the most commonly transmitted pet diseases. Cats and dogs can carry roundworms and excrete the eggs in their feces. Children are often infected after playing with animals, or touching their droppings, and then putting their hands in their mouths. The roundworm larvae can travel to the liver, muscles, eyes or central nervous system. Symptoms mimic the flu: fever, cough, congestion, weakness and loss of appetite. To prevent roundworms, have animals examined by a veterinarian, and keep young children away from animal droppings. Covering sandboxes when not in use can lessen the chances of animals leaving droppings in the sand.

Cat Scratch Fever

Swollen lymph nodes, high fever, loss of appetite and weakness can indicate cat scratch fever, a generally mild infection which may or may not be associated with a cat scratch. Very deep scratches could mean a serious but rare infection from Pasteurella bacterium. Almost every cat and nearly half the dogs in the U.S. harbor this bacteria in their mouths. Pasteurella poisoning can destroy tissues near the scratch, and infect bones and blood. Penicillin treatment after any deep scratch or bite is usually recommended by doctors to prevent these ill effects.

Strep Throat, Pet Throat?

Repeated bouts of strep throat are common for some families, but they may be suffering unnecessarily. A New York doctor recently found that 40 percent of the pets in families stricken with strep throat were carrying active strep organisms, though the animals showed no symptoms. Treating the animals with antibiotics ended the recurring strep throats in children.

Notes
1. United States Department of Agriculture, Food Safety and Inspection Service
2. *Accident Facts,* National Safety Council 1984)
3. Ibid.

Chapter Three
Risks on the Job

Most of us spend a substantial portion of our lives at work. This chapter will look at the risks of injury, disease and stress in different occupations.

 The Pink and White Collar Blues

The more we learn about the dangers of stress and the sedentary life, the more we see that occupations such as firefighting and mining are not the only risky professions. The overweight, coffee-gulping executive or the telephone operator whose performance is monitored by a computer may have as high a risk of hypertension and heart disease as a construction worker has of more sudden injury.

Despite the carpeting and air conditioning, a secretary's job may be far from "cushy." Eighteen million pink collar workers—secretaries, clerks, data processors, telephone operators and others—make up the largest occupational group in the U.S. Eighty percent of these workers are women. The National Institute of Occupational Safety and Health (NIOSH) has found that pink collar workers have a disturbingly high rate of coronary heart disease.

If you have little control on your job, if your work is repetitive or you feel you are not using your skills to the fullest, you probably feel stressed. A NIOSH survey which rated the stress level of different occupations found that the most stressful occupations involved long hours, low pay, little recognition, and a pace set by a machine or superior. Journalists, professors, craftspeople, and politicians may also experience stress on the job, but they generally areinvolved in varied activities utilizing several skills, can pace themselves and can exercise some degree of control over the direction of their work. Similarly, doctors, lawyers and executives may work under a lot of pressure, but the control they have over how they deal with their workloads, as well as their higher salaries and recognition, appear to offset some of the negative effects of stress.

Cashiers, garment stitchers, telephone operators, food-service workers, and inspection workers all have jobs which can be high on demand but low on control. While many of us might consider the top executive overloaded with decisions as the prime candidate for stress-related heart disease, researchers at Columbia University have found that jobs requiring little decision-making could be as hard on the heart as high cholesterol or cigarette smoking.

 **The Computer Age**

Ideally we use computers to make our lives easier, yet for some people they cause anxiety, boredom and even ill health. About 10 million Americans use video display terminals (VDT's) daily. Clerical workers who use VDT's experience more stress, boredom and fatigue than workers doing equivalent work on conventional typewriters, according to a NIOSH study. VDT users who spend a lot of their day in front of the screen can suffer from eyestrain, irritated eyes, headaches and blurred vision. A study by the National Association of Women Office Workers found that 60 percent of all VDT users experience eye problems. Often office lighting creates too much glare on the screen, making users more prone to eye strain. VDT's should be viewed in a dimly lit room to allow for sharp contrast between the characters and the screen.

Recently, two office workers unions testified before Congress that VDT's may be responsible for abnormally high rates of miscarriage, stillbirth and other pregnancy problems in 23 different groups of working women. Half of the pregnant women had miscarriages, stillbirths or babies with birth defects, which is more than double the normal rate. NIOSH is investigating the problem, and although there is no hard evidence yet, VDT users who become pregnant would be prudent to transfer to other jobs.

Some workers are monitored by a computer which keeps track of their errors and production rates, creating an antagonistic atmosphere and a lot of unhealthy stress. The National Center for Health Statistics studied telephone operators whosit within inches of each other, and have to handle a call in no more than 15 seconds after which another call is immediately put through. Their work is constantly monitored by a computer. The operators had three times the amount of chest pain as people who have "high-control" jobs.

The Envelope Please...

The NIOSH study of stress-related occupations named some of the following as the most likely to cause stress-related illness: laborers, secretaries, inspectors (such as chicken inspectors), lab technicians, office managers, foremen, administrators, waiters and waitresses, machine operators, farm owners, mine workers, house painters, health technologists, nurses, dental assistants, social workers, computer programmers, bank tellers, teacher's aides, telephone operators, sales managers, sales representatives, policemen, firemen, electricians, plumbers, machinists, hairdressers.

Cancer on the job

The National Institute of Occupational Safety and Health (NIOSH) estimates that 40 to 50 million Americans, almost a quarter of the population, have been exposed to hazardous chemicals in the workplace. Asbestos, arsenic, benzene, chromium and nickel are a few chemicals commonly used in the workplace which are known to cause cancer. Anyone whose occupation involves working with these substances, such as miners, oil refiners, printers, shoemakers, battery makers, glass and pottery workers, and textile workers, to some degree risk developing cancer or other diseases.

■ People who work near powerful electrical or magnetic fields, such as electricians, radio and television repairmen, power-station operators, subway drivers and aluminum workers, may have an increased risk of developing leukemia, according to the Washington State Department of Social and Health Services. Aluminum workers exposed to magnetic fields from electric currents 250 times stronger than a car battery's had double the number of leukemia deaths as the general population.

■ In a study of workers most likely to develop lung cancer, the Harvard School of Public of Health found that truck drivers, cooks, steel workers, asbestos workers, painters, auto mechanics, fleet fishermen, heated metal workers, brick and stone masons, and tile setters were all 29 to 43 percent more likely to die of lung cancer than the general population. Plumbers and sheet metal workers had a 22 percent greater risk. Truck drivers, for example, breathe a lot of engine exhaust, and steel workers are exposed to coke oven emissions. The carcinogen which puts cooks at a higher risk is not known.

■ Industrial workers are not the only ones exposed to carcinogens. Office workers may breathe asbestos from the air conditioning and heating systems. Hairdressers may risk lung cancer by inhaling fumes from hair sprays and hair dyes. Dry cleaners and machinists exposed to carbon tetrachloride may develop liver cancer. In one case, meat cutters developing symptoms of asthma were found to be using machines that released polyvinyl chloride fumes. Hospital workers are exposed to toxic chemicals in disinfectants, bacteriocides, laboratory materials and laundry substances.

The list of workers exposed to carcinogens is long and varied, and the risks are difficult to assess numerically, as people are exposed more than one carcinogen, both on and off the job. If you believe your job exposes you to any hazardous material, see the suggestions at the end of this chapter.

Physical Injury and Death

Firefighters lead all other occupations in deaths per 100,000 workers:[1]

Occupation	Deaths
Firefighting	58
Mining	55
Agriculture	54
Construction	40
Transportation	31
Police	23
All industries	12
Government	10
Manufacturing	7
Services	7
Trades	5

Of the 4,090 work-related deaths recorded in 1982 (for establishments with 11 workers or more), nearly 30 percent were caused by car and truck accidents.

Injury rates are highest in establishments with 100 to 249 employees, and lowest in establishments with fewer than 50 workers or more than 1,000. Mining establishments have the highest number of average lost workdays per injury—25 days. Construction, transportation and public utilities industries also have high numbers of lost workdays.[2]

As your age increases, so do your odds of becoming injured on the job. More than 2.5 million workers were disabled on the job in 1983. The chances of being disabled for a year or longer:

Age	Odds
18 to 34	1 in 1,000
35 to 49	3 in 1,000
50 to 54	6 in 1,000
55 to 62	15 in 1,000

Source: Health Insurance Association of America

What to do?

You have a right to a safe workplace. If you believe your work involves unsafe conditions, you can take steps to improve it:

1. Talk to your co-workers to determine how many share ailments such as respiratory problems, eyestrain, headaches or reproductive difficulties. If workers are suffering a lot of stress, suggest to your employer that employees rotate tasks for variety, and be allowed to participate in decisions concerning the pace of their work. (A sample questionnaire for employees is available from the Occupational Health and Safety Project, 100 Arlington St., Room 228, Boston, MA, 02116.)

2. Obtain the chemical names of the materials you work with, and ask your employer whether they are monitored. Note fumes, dusts, gases, noise, ventilation, radiation and lighting. Discuss the hazard with your employer and see if you can settle on a solution.

3. Research the latest protective clothing and equipment for use in your occupation. Have suggestions ready, such as non-skid carpeting, alternative disposal of waste products, improved lighting, etc. Union members should follow the appropriate grievance procedures.

4. The National Institute for Occupational Safety and Health (NIOSH) can perform a health hazard evaluation if your employer is uncooperative. You and two other employees must make a written request. Write to NIOSH, 4676 Columbia Parkway, Cincinnati, OH 45226.

5. Do not continue to work under unsafe conditions. The Supreme Court upholds your right to refuse to work under conditions you

reasonably believe could cause serious injury or death. If you lose your job, you can file a complaint with the Occupational Safety and Health Administration.

Notes
1. International Firefighters Association
2. Bureau of Labor Statistics

Chapter Four
Transportation Risks: Which Way to Go is the Safest?

  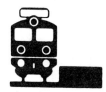

Based on death rate per passenger mile, the safest way to travel is by commercial airliner or by train. Depending on the year studied trains and large planes are the safest travel mode. It is 25 to 30 times safer to travel by commercial jet than by passenger car. Travel by small aircraft (private planes, general aviation), however is four times as dangerous as driving. Flying by commuter airliner is seven times as dangerous as flying in a larger plane, but is still four times as safe as driving.

Driving a truck is safer, by a small amount, than driving a car. Driving a large car, preferably a station wagon, is roughly as safe as driving a truck.

Riding a bus is three times as safe as a passenger car. Intercity buses are safer per mile than urban buses.

Walking is 10-20 times as dangerous as driving. Motorcycles are eleven and a half times as dangerous as cars. Bicycles are about as dangerous as motorcycles.

If all these statistics make you want to stay at home, the rest of this chapter will explain how you can travel more safely.

How Safe Is It?

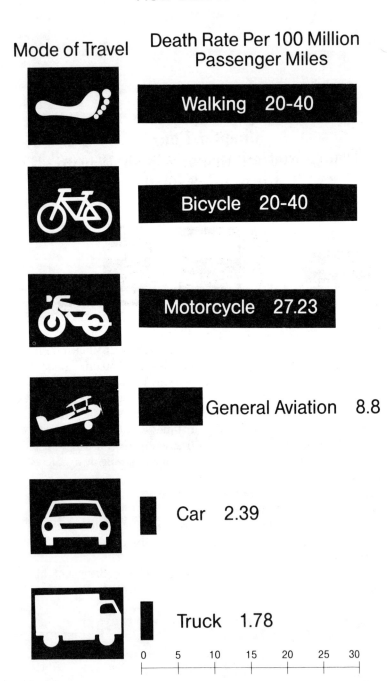

Mode of Travel	Death Rate Per 100 Million Passenger Miles
🦶	Walking 20-40
🚲	Bicycle 20-40
🏍️	Motorcycle 27.23
✈️	General Aviation 8.8
🚗	Car 2.39
🚚	Truck 1.78

0   5   10   15   20   25   30

42

Mode of Travel

Death Rate Per 100 Million Passenger Miles

Bus   0.87

Commuter Airline   0.35-0.70

Intercity Bus   0.35

Local Rail Transit   0.14

Major Airline   0.08-0.10

Train   0.07

| 0.10 | 0.20 | 0.30 | 0.40 | 0.50 | 0.60 | 0.70 | 0.80 | 0.90 | 1.0 |

Cars

The average driver is involved in one car accident every five years. One out of every fourteen accidents is a serious one. Three out of four accidents occur within 25 miles of home, and 80% of serious injuries and deaths occur in cars traveling 40 miles per hour or less.

The United States is one of the safest nations to drive a car in, per mile of driving. For 1980 the fatality rates for major nations:

Country	Fatalities per 100 million vehicle miles
Norway	3.0
U.S.	3.5
Finland	3.6
United Kingdom	3.7
Denmark	4.1
Canada	4.3
Japan	4.8
Australia	4.9
Netherlands	5.3
Italy	6.6
Germany	6.7
France	7.3
Belgium	8.6
Spain	12.1

Source: National Safety Council.

Reducing Auto Risks

Fatality rates are caused by many factors: traffic density, crash-worthiness of vehicles, design of roads, skills and training of drivers, alcohol laws, seatbelt laws, speed limits and customs.

There are four basic strategies for reducing the risk that you will be injured in a car accident. First of all you should always wear a seat belt. Only 12 to 14% of Americans wear seatbelts. Experts believe that at least one-half of highway deaths would be eliminated if people would wear seat belts. Only two percent of those who died in traffic accidents in United States were wearing seatbelts.

In 1985 New York State became the first state in the U.S. to require seatbelts to be worn. Before the law was enacted seat belt usage in New York was about 15%. The month before the law went into effect 62% of drivers and passengers wore belts. The month that the law went into effect usage increased to 88%.

In 1972 Australia became the first country to require seatbelt usage,

44

and its automobile accident death rate has been reduced dramatically. Eighty-seven percent of Australians currently use their seat belts. In the first two years of mandatory seat belt law in Australia, facial injuries were cut in half and spinal injuries fell by one-third. The auto death rate has been cut by 20% there and serious injuries have been reduced by 30 percent.

In Sweden severe and fatal injuries have been reduced by 45% for drivers and 67% for passengers after passage of a seat belt law in 1975. Fully 85% of Swedes wear seat belts.

In the seven Canadian provinces where seat belt use is mandatory, highway deaths have been reduced by from 3.5% to 24%.

The second strategy for reducing highway risks is to drive a safer car. The appendix to this chapter includes safety ratings for most cars. Even if you don't buy a newer car, you can make your vehicle safer by installing midline brake lights. These lights are mounted in the middle of the car behind the back window. Research has shown that front-into-rear collisions are cut in half when the midline brake lights are used. The cost of these lights is about $15.00.

Another technique for reducing your risk of auto accidents is to drive defensively by driving more slowly, and by anticipating accident-causing situations. Obviously, don't drink alcoholic beverages if you are planning to drive. Try to anticipate possible accidents. Be prepared for:

- sudden stops of driver in front of you;
- drivers to cut in front of you;
- cars entering intersections without stopping;
- pedestrians darting out.

Don't change lanes constantly. Keep your speed constant and keep a safe distance behind the car in front of you (two car lengths per 10 miles per hour). Never back up in traffic or when you missed your exit. Your chances of having an accident when backing up on a highway are about fifty-fifty.

The final strategy for reducing the risks of driving is to drive less often, especially during snow and rain storms. You can either stay at home, or, take a commercial airliner, train or a bus. Since night driving is more dangerous than daytime driving you can reduce the amount you drive after sundown.

Men and Women Drivers

Male drivers are twice as likely to be involved in traffic accidents as women. This is because men drive about twice as many miles as women do. Per mile male and female accident rates are nearly identical. According to the National Safety Council men have 19.8 accidents per million miles of driving, while women have 18.6 accidents per million miles. In the United States in 1982 male drivers were involved in 20.6 million motor vehicle accidents while women were involved in 9.9 million collisions.

Night and Daytime Driving

Sixteen year old males are four times as likely to be killed in a car accident at night as during the daylight hours. For sixteen-year-old females the ratio is three to one. For all drivers your chances for being killed when driving at night is three to four times the risk of death during daytime.

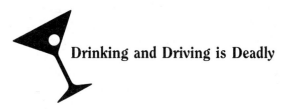 **Drinking and Driving is Deadly**

On a typical weekend evening one out of every ten cars coming toward you is driven by a drunk driver. On Sunday through Thursday night one out of 50 drivers is drunk. About half of the highway fatalities in the United States are alcohol-related. Thirty-five percent of those alcohol-related fatalities were in the 16-24 age group.

Age and Auto Accidents

Drivers' Age	Fatal accidents per 100,000 drivers
under 20	54
20-24	72
25-29	45
30-34	40
35-39	29
40-44	33
45-49	26
50-54	19
55-59	20
60-64	23
65-69	21
70-74	23
75 and over	55

Source: National Safety Council.

Teenage drivers cause five times as many highway deaths as drivers in the 35-64 age group. But teenagers are not the most dangerous drivers. Drivers from age twenty to twenty-four are the most deadly. The safest drivers are in their early 50's. Drivers over age 75 are as dangerous as teenagers.

Big Cars, Small Cars

As you might expect you are generally safer when driving a big car than driving a smaller one. There are two reasons for this. First, you have more crash protection in a big car. Secondly, small cars are tailgated more often than large cars. According to Purdue University's Automotive Transportation Center small cars are tailgated more frequently and are involved in 18% more rear-end collisions than large cars. Thomas Sparrow, the director of the Center, said that larger vehicles tend to creep up on small cars because the consequences of hitting a small car are not as great. He added that some drivers tailgate smaller cars because they perceive them as being farther away.

Injury Rates for Various Cars

Make of Auto	Station wagon	4-Door	2-Door
Chevrolet Cavalier	87	109	129
Ford Escort	93	113	121
Chevrolet Caprice	65	76	85
Honda Accord	—	86	102
Olds Delta 88	—	59	69
Plymouth Reliant K	90	104	112
Suburu	99	127	125
Toyota Corolla	106	132	140
Volvo	70	91	113

Source: Highway Loss Data Institute.

These statistics are based on 1982/83 data for model year 1981-1983 cars. The complete list of cars and their injury risks are included at the end of this chapter.

If you are considering the purchase of a small car, consider a small station wagon. The wagon model of smaller cars is significantly safer than the sedan model. There is also statistical significance to the difference between two and four door models of the smaller cars. This difference may be attributed to the type of person who buys these cars rather than inherent safeness. Two-door models are considered to be more sporty and may attracted wilder drivers.

Station wagons are safer than four-door sedans and four door sedans are safer than two door models. The table below is based on actual accident data. The average car had an injury rating of 100. The lower the number the safer the car.

Better Bumpers Mean Safer Cars

For 1983-model-year cars the U.S. government reduced the bumper standard. This allowed manufacturers to use "2 1/2 mile-per-hour" bumpers instead of the "5 mile-per-hour" bumpers which were required for 1982-model year cars. A "five-mile-per-hour" bumper will prevent damage in five mile-per-hour crashes. Some manufacturers still use the stronger bumpers. Cars with the stronger bumpers give passengers more protection against injury and reduce damage when cars are involved in accidents.

Are Rag Tops Risky?

Are convertibles safe to drive? U.S. lawmakers considered banning the rag-top cars in the 1970's, but never did so. Because there are few convertibles on the road data is somewhat limited. The Volkswagen Rabbit convertible has been on the U.S. market for over five years. Surprisingly the VW Rabbit convertible has shown itself to be safer than the two model, about as safe as the four door Rabbit.

In addition to the actual accident data previously referred to, the U.S. government conducts crash tests. In these tests, vehicles driven by mechanical "dummies" are crashed into concrete barriers. Convertibles usually fared worse than hardtop versions of the same cars in crash tests. However, in these tests passengers usually were less injured in convertibles than in hardtops, while for drivers the results were the opposite.

If a convertible turns over injuries can be severe. However, most convertibles have a lower center of gravity than sedans, and thus are less likely to overturn in an accident. The exception is 4-wheel drive vehicles, such as jeeps, which have a high center of gravity.

The data is inconsistent, but it is reasonable to conclude that convertibles are not significantly more dangerous than cars of a similar size and weight.

Where You Drive Makes a Difference

We all know that "LA is a great big freeway" but it is only the second city in traffic deaths. Houston leads the county in traffic fatalities per 100,000 people (20.3). Los Angeles comes in a distant second at 13.8. By comparison, cities more dependent on public transportation like New York, Chicago and Philadelphia, have highway fatality rates of between 7 and 8 per 100,000 residents.

Motorcycles, Mopeds and All-Terrain Vehicles

If you ride a motorcycle you are 11 1/2 times more likely to be involved in a fatal accident as a motorist. There are about 5,000 motorcycle fatalities per year in the United States. While there are more motor vehicle deaths, motorists put on more miles. In California 1.5% of all 18 year old males are injured in motorcycle accidents every year.

Moped riders not wearing helmets are nine times more likely to be killed if an accident occurs than riders who wear the protective headgear, according to the *Annals of Emergency Medicine*. In addition to wearing a helmet cyclists can reduce injuries by wearing leather clothing. If you are involved in an accident leather will be scraped from you jacket or pants, protecting your skin.

All-terrain cycles, three-wheeled motorbikes, have a great risk of overturning because of their high center of gravity. These cycles are increasing rapidly in popularity, and unfortunately, so is the death rate of ATC users. Almost three-quarters of the injuries related to these vehicles were to riders between ages five and 24, and one-third involved children under age 15. The hospitalization rate of these cycles is twice the rate for minibikes and trailbikes. Of all the vehicles studied, all-terrain cycles are the least safe at any speed. Safety experts recommend that ATC should not be used.

Bicycling

More than 900 bicyclists are killed on U.S. streets every year. While the exact number of miles ridden by bicycle can only be estimated, the evidence indicates that bicycling is very dangerous, on a par with motorcycling. Most bicycle accident victims are children under 16 years of age, and in most cases the bicyclist was the cause of the accident.

Precautions you can take to avoid injuries:

- wear a hard-shell helmet;
- ride on the right-side of the road and as near to the right edge as possible;
- use lighting and light or reflective clothing at night;
- watch out for parked as well as moving vehicles. A suddenly opened car door can be disastrous;
- ride on bike paths or designated bike routes, if possible; and
- watch out for dogs; outrun them if you can, but dogs sometimes run in front of your wheels.

Walk Carefully!

About 8,000 pedestrians are killed by traffic in the United States annually. Based on an average pedestrian mileage of 1/4 to 1/2 mile per day this makes walking one of the most dangerous means of transportation. (The only studies available are for England, where pedestrians averaged slightly more than 1/2 mile per day; since the U.S. is more motorized than England a lower figure was used). In any event it is clear that walking in urbanized areas is at least ten times as dangerous as driving.

About three-fourths of the pedestrians killed are young children, the elderly or under the influence of alcohol. Walking at night is more dangerous than during the daylight hours. Pedestrians have to walk "defensively" to avoid accidents:

■ anticipate actions of drivers;
■ wear visible clothing at night;
■ don't walk if you have been drinking (don't drive either — take a taxi)
■ don't walk between parked cars or jaywalk.

Flying the Safe and Friendly Skies

In 1983 more Americans died from bee stings than from airplane accidents involving major air lines. It is 30 times safer than traveling by car. Scheduled commuter airline travel is seven times more dangerous than flying a major carrier. And flying in commuter planes with ten or fewer seats is more than twice as dangerous as flying in large commuter aircraft.

However, flying by any scheduled airline is safer than driving. Flying in small private aircraft is far more dangerous than driving a car.

APPENDIX: WHICH CARS ARE THE SAFEST?

[100 represents the average risk of injury: the lower the number the safer the car is]

Model	Station Wagon Injury		4-door Injury		2-door Injury	
	Overall	Severe	Overall	Severe	Overall	Severe
AMC						
CONCORD	95		105			
EAGLE	75				89	
SPIRIT					127	117
AUDI						
4000			97			
5000			84	100		
BUICK						
CENTURY			83	79	95	
ELECTRA			69	78	83	
LE SABRE			62	62	79	97
REGAL	62		78	73	88	94
RIVIERA					73	77
SKYHAWK			115	116		
SKYLARK			87	78	94	95
BMW 320i					93	105
CADILLAC						
BROUGHAM			78	94	79	
CIMARRON			88			
DE VILLE			67	81	84	100
ELDORADO					80	106
SEVILLE			72	78		
CHEVROLET						
CAMARO					113	126
CAPRICE	65	60	76	81	85	
CAVALIER	87	86	109	113	129	132
CELEBRITY			91	79	96	
CHEVETTE			127	125	142	146
CITATION			97	90		
CORVETTE					93	113
IMPALA			76	80		
MALIBU	77	74	91	88		
MONTE CARLO					100	115
CHRYSLER						
CORDOBA					79	86
LE BARON			87	83	94	
NEW YORKER			69	79		

DATSUN/NISSAN

200SX					132	135
280ZX					108	124
810	90		113	125		
PULSAR					148	
SENTRA	99		140			
STANZA			110	106	106	

DODGE

ARIES-K	87	83	104	95	104	108
COLT					148	145
DIPLOMAT			75			
MIRADA					112	
OMNI			113	101	132	126

FORD

CROWN VICTORIA	66		69	77	66	
ESCORT	93	89	113	109	121	120
EXP					123	127
FUTURA			106	100	106	104
LTD			97			
MUSTANG					121	123
THUNDERBIRD					92	

HONDA

ACCORD			86	87	102	104
CIVIC			114	116	121	111

ISUZU I-MARK

			128			

LINCOLN

CONTINENTAL			65			
MARK VI			86		68	
TOWN CAR			72	84		

MAZDA

GLC			122	103	111	105
RX-7					101	92

MERCEDES

240D			67			
300D			69			
300SD			61			

MERCURY

CAPRI					121	124
LN7					110	
LYNX	86	71	113	120	124	
GRAND MARQUIS	68		66	67	96	
ZEPHYR			115		121	

	1	2	3	4	5	6
OLDSMOBILE						
CIERRA			86	74	95	
CUSTOM						
CRUISER	61					
CUTLASS	60	44	76	70	88	90
DELTA 88			59	58	69	73
98			60	74	72	
OMEGA			90	85	95	96
PEUGEOT 505			85			
PLYMOUTH						
HORIZON			111	105	126	119
RELIANT-K	90	76	104	92	112	110
SAPPORO				145		
PONTIAC						
1000			127		156	145
2000	85		104		111	94
6000			92	85		
BONNEVILLE	69	60	79	78		
FIREBIRD					112	115
GRAND PRIX					90	96
PHOENIX			94	86		
RENAULT						
ALLIANCE					133	
LE CAR						
(RENAULT 5)					144	
SAAB 900			69		77	
SUBARU						
GL/DL 4WD	97	103			110	
DL/GL	98	94	127	129		
HARDTOP					141	143
HATCHBACK					125	118
TOYOTA						
CELICA					123	131
CELICA SUPRA					98	
COROLLA	106	104	132	140	140	145
CRESSIDA			91	120		
TERCEL			132		133	
VOLKSWAGEN						
JETTA			85		75	
RABBIT			92	88	98	97
RABBIT						
CONVERTIBLE					95	
VOLVO	70		91	105	113	

Chapter Five

The Perils of Eros:
Sex Risks

The road to *amour* is pocked with risks, some more traumatic than anything your mother might have warned you about. If the adventure of sex is one of life's greatest thrills, its price is an assortment of threats to one's emotional, psychological and physical well-being. Sexual revolution or not, when we engage in sex, we are in one of our most vulnerable states.

Sexually Transmitted Diseases
Chlamydia: Known by Few, Had by Many

What is the leading sexually transmitted disease in America? Although news stories about herpes and AIDS abound, the most common venereal disease receives little press coverage. Three to ten million Americans suffer from genital chlamydia each year, five times the number of gonorrhea cases. Chlamydia causes about 20,000 cases of pelvic inflammatory disease (PID)—a major cause of sterility in women. Pelvic inflammatory disease can also cause tubal pregnancies (see Pregnancy chapter), responsible for eleven percent of all maternal deaths.

Chlamydia can cause miscarriage, low birthweight, and infant death. Infants may be contaminated with a chlamydial infection at birth and suffer eye infections and pneumonia. Studies at the Center for Disease Control reveal that about half of the cases of pneumonia in infants under eight weeks old are caused by chlamydial infections picked up from their mothers.

Chlamydia is spread through sexual intercourse. Men usually show symptoms of whitish discharge from penis and itching or burning during urination within one to five weeks of infection. Women may have a vaginal discharge, fever, stomach pain or burning sensation during urination, or *they may not have any symptoms at all.* Chlamy-

54

dia in a symptomless woman means her disease can go undiagnosed, increasing the chances of injury to herself and spreading the disease to others.

Chlamydia is treated with antibiotics. Both partners should be treated at the same time.

Gonorrhea

After the common cold, gonorrhea is the most widespread communicable disease, infecting 250 million people worldwide each year, and about three million in the U.S. Males usually experience symptoms—severe burning while urinating and a yellowish discharge—within two to ten days of exposure. Up to 80 percent of infected women and small percentage of men notice no symptoms at all, making it vital for infected males with symptoms to notify all their sexual partners

Gonorrhea is treated with antibiotics. Some strains of gonorrhea have become resistant to certain antibiotics, so it is important for the patient to be tested for gonorrhea again one week after treatment. Left untreated, gonorrhea can lead to blood infections, arthritis, and pelvic infections in women which can cause sterility.

Herpes

Genital herpes afflicts about one in 22 Americans. About 300,000 *new* cases of herpes arise each year. Although herpes rarely causes serious physical harm, no cure has been found. The primary herpes infection generally lasts a few weeks, then the virus remains dormant in nerve cells until something triggers another outbreak.

The symptoms of genital herpes are small fluid-filled blisters on the genitals which can be quite painful and may be accompanied by fever, irritability and fatigue. Recurrences usually result in less painful sores which heal more quickly. Recurrences are generally triggered by injury or rubbing of the skin, sexual intercourse, menstruation, fever, or emotional stress. People with an active herpes infection should avoid touching their eyes. Any woman who has had herpes should get regular Pap smears, as genital herpes infection has been linked with a later development of cervical cancer.

Herpes and the Newborn

About one in 7,000 babies born in the United States is born with herpes. Two-thirds of the infected babies die from the disease, while half of those who survive suffer serious damage, such as meningitis, encephalitis and brain damage. Cesarean sections are usually recommended to mothers with active herpes at the time of delivery.

AIDS

Nearly 9,000 Americans have contracted AIDS, the venereal disease which attacks the body's immune system, making victims vulnerable to life-threatening infections or cancer. About three-fourths of the people who contracted AIDS before 1983 have died.

Homosexual or bisexual men account for three-fourths of the total cases. Intravenous drug users, Haitians, and hemophiliacs are also high risk groups, and can pass the disease to their sexual contacts. One percent of the total cases can be traced to blood transfusions. A very small number of medical technicians who handle AIDS infected blood have contracted the disease.

The World Health Organization has declared AIDS epidemic in France, Denmark, Switzerland, Great Britain, West Germany and Belgium. AIDS is not just a homosexual disease. Sexually active heterosexuals, especially those living in big cities, may also be vulnerable to AIDS.

STD'S: Who's most at risk?

Teenagers and young adults run a significantly higher risk of contracting a sexually transmitted disease than their older counterparts. The highest incidence of gonorrhea is found in the 20-24 age group, with 15-19 year olds a close second. Amongst all sexually active people, about one in ten has some form of a venereal disease.

Prevention involves careful screening of potential partners and the use of condoms, particularly with new sex partners. Early treatment also cuts down on risks, as many of the diseases respond to antibiotics.

The incidence of STD's among homosexual men is much higher than that of the general population both because of the type of sexual activity preferred (oral/genital, penile/anal, or oral/anal) and the increased exposure to multiple partners. One study reported that 75 percent of surveyed gay men in San Francisco claimed to have over 100 different sexual partners over a lifetime. Because the sexual encounters often take place in anonymous situations such as bathhouses, it can be difficult to locate infected partners.

Lesbians, however, have less of a risk of catching a STD than either gay men or heterosexual women. Partly this reduced risk is due to preferred lovemaking techniques, which range from cunnilingus to manual manipulation of genitals. Non-use of both intrauterine devices, which increase susceptibility to pelvic inflammatory disease and vaginitis, and contraceptives, which tend to encourage yeast infections, also cut the risk.

Heterosexual women who have had intercourse at an early age, many different male partners or given birth a number of times are also more susceptible to cervical cancer than homosexual women. The sexual revolution in Great Britain has been blamed for a startling increase in cases of cervical cancer, as more girls lose their virginity in their early teens. Cervical cancer is practically never seen in nuns, who usually do not engage in sexual intercourse at any age. Low rates of cervical cancer have also been observed in members of the Old Order Amish, the Mormons, and the Seventh-Day Adventists. Researchers note that Protestant and Catholic women who regularly attend church, as well as Jewish, Irish, Italian and Moslem immigrant women, have lower cervical cancer rates than Protestant and Catholic women who rarely or never attend services, and than Puerto Rican, black and Mexican immigrant women.[1] The implication of that observation is left to the reader.

Barrier methods of contraception, such as the condom and diaphragm, may protect against this cancer. The simple Pap test, a cervical smear, can detect if a woman is prone to the disease, which can then be cured if caught in its early stages.

Years of Decline?

A waning of sexual interest occurs in both sexes as couples grow old together. A study[2] of the elderly with an average age of 59 showed that six percent of the men and 33 percent of the women no longer had any interest in sex, and 12 percent of the men and 44 percent of the women no longer engaged in intercourse (which means that half of the men and a quarter of the women who no longer have sex are still interested in it.)

About two out of three men in their early sixties are still sexually active; the figures drop to one in five when a man reaches his eighties. One third of the women in their sixties are still interested in sex, but only a fifth   are sexually active, undoubtedly because of women's greater longevity. Nearly half of the women surveyed gave death, separation or divorce from spouse as reasons for the lack of sexual activity. For those women who continued to live with their husbands but who no longer had sexual intercourse, forty percent of the men and eighteen percent of the women attributed the ending of sexual activity to the man's inability to perform sexually. Only six percent of the men and four percent of the women believed that the woman's inability to function sexually was to blame. Sex lives also end when a partner becomes ill—about one-third of the men and over one-fifth of the women cited this reason.

For those continuing to be sexually active, frequency of intercourse drops with age. Most men aged 46 to 50 report having intercourse once a week; from 66 to 71, a little over half made love once a month. Women 46 to 50 are equally divided among those having sex once a month, once a week, or twice a week or more. Most women 66 to 71 are no longer sexually active.

Contraception

When choosing contraception, a couple must juggle the risk of pregnancy against the side effects of the particular method. No method is 100 percent effective. The following outline compares the effectiveness and health risks of the different kinds of birth control methods.

The Pill

"The Pill" refers to any of the oral contraceptives. Today, approximately 10 to 12 million women use birth control pills in the U.S. One to two million of those women, however, are unsuitable candidates for this method of birth control. Women who want to use the pill should be aware of factors which may put them at greater risk, some of which follow.

Effectiveness: Effectiveness depends on how correctly the method is used. Of 100 women who use the combination estrogen and progestin pill for one year, less than one will become pregnant. Of 100 women who use the progestin-only pill (mini-pill) for one year, two to three will become pregnant.

Advantages: The combination pill, which contains both estrogen and progestin, is the most effective of the popular methods for preventing pregnancy. No inconvenient devices to bother with at time of intercourse.

Disadvantages: Must be taken regularly and exactly as instructed by the prescribing physician.

Side Effects: On the positive side, oral contraceptives can diminish the severity of menstrual cramps, and reduce the amount of blood lost in the menstrual cycle, lessening the chance of iron deficiency. Women on the pill are also less likely to develop ovarian cysts. Acne improves in some women, although it worsens in others.

On the down side, pill users may experience tender breasts, nausea or vomiting, gain or loss of weight, unexpected vaginal bleeding, and higher levels of sugar and fat in the blood.

Some women notice that their contact lenses no longer fit because the shape of the cornea has been changed by estrogen-related fluid retention.

Although it happens infrequently, use of The Pill can cause blood clots (in the legs, and less frequently in the lungs, brain, and heart). A clot that reaches the lungs or forms in the brain or heart can be fatal. Pill users have a greater risk of heart attack and stroke than non-users. This risk increases with age and is greater if the Pill user smokes.

Some Pill users tend to develop high blood pressure, but it usually is mild and may be reversed by discontinuing use.

Pill users have a greater risk than non-users of having gall bladder disease requiring surgery.

Rarely, benign liver tumors occur in women on The Pill. Sometimes they rupture, causing fatal hemorrhage.

Health factors to consider: Women who use The Pill are strongly advised not to smoke because smoking increases the risk of heart attack or stroke.

Other women who should not take The Pill are those who have had a heart attack, stroke, angina pectoris, blood clots, cancer of the breast or uterus. Women who have scanty or irregular periods should be encouraged to use some other method.

A woman who believes she may be pregnant should not take The Pill becauses it increases the risk of defect in the fetus.

Health problems, such as migraine headaches, mental depression, fibroids of the uterus, heart or kidney disease, asthma, high blood pressure, diabetes, or epilepsy may be made worse by use of The Pill.

Risks associated with The Pill increase for women as they get older. The death rate for younger pill users is about five women in 100,000. The mortality rate increases the older the woman is and the longer she uses the pill. For women who have used The Pill continuously for five or more years, the mortality rate is about one death in 2,000 women per year, which is greater than the risk of death from pregnancy.

Warning Signs for Pill Users: All of the dangerous complications of pill use are preceded by one or more of the following symptoms: abdominal pain, headaches, eye problems (blurred vision, spots in front of the eyes), leg pain and chest pain. See a doctor immediately if you experience any of these danger signals, and always tell any doctor you see for any reason that you are taking birth control pills.

Long-term effects on ability to have children: There is no evidence that using The Pill will prevent a woman from becoming pregnant after she stops taking it, although there may be a delay before she is able to become pregnant. Women should wait a short time after stopping The Pill before becoming pregnant, using another method of contraception in the meantime.

After childbirth the woman should consult her doctor before resuming use of The Pill. This is especially true for nursing mothers because the drugs in The Pill appear in the milk and the long-range effect on the infant is not known. The Pill may also cause nursing mothers to produce less milk.

Intrauterine device (IUD)

The IUD is a small plastic or metal device that is placed in the uterus (womb) through the cervical canal (opening into the uterus). As long as the IUD stays in place, pregnancy is prevented. How the IUD prevents pregnancy is not completely understood. IUD's seem to interfere in some manner with implantation of the fertilized egg in the wall of the uterus. IUD's containing copper should be replaced every three years; those containing progesterone should be replaced every year.

Approximately three to four million women use the IUD in the U.S.

Effectiveness: Effectiveness depends on proper insertion by the physician and whether the IUD remains in place. Of 100 women who use an IUD for one year, one to six will become pregnant.

Advantages: Insertion by a physician, then no further care needed, except to see that the IUD remains in place (the user can check it herself but should be checked once a year by a doctor).

Disadvantages: May cause pain or discomfort when inserted; afterward may cause cramps and a heavier menstrual flow. Some women will experience adverse effects that require removal of the IUD. The IUD can be expelled, sometimes without the woman being aware of it, leaving her unprotected.

Side Effects: Major complications, which are infrequent, include anemia, pregnancy outside the uterus, pelvic infection, perforation of the uterus or cervix, and abortion.

The IUD causes menstrual periods to last longer, increasing the risk of iron deficiency anemia. A woman with heavy or irregular bleeding while using an IUD should consult her doctor. Removal of the IUD may be necessary to prevent anemia.

Women susceptible to pelvic infection are more prone to infection when using an IUD.

Serious complications can occur if a woman becomes pregnant while using an IUD. Though rare, cases of blood poisoning, miscarriage, and even death have been reported. An IUD user who believes she may be pregnant should consult her doctor immediately. If pregnancy is confirmed, the IUD should be removed.

The IUD may sometimes pierce the wall of the uterus when it is being inserted. Surgery is required to remove it.

Health factors to consider: Before having an IUD inserted, a woman should tell her doctor if she has had any of the following: cancer or other abnormalities of the uterus or cervix; bleeding between periods or heavy menstrual flow; infection of the uterus, cervix, or pelvis; prior IUD use; recent pregnancy, abortion, or miscarriage; uterine surgery; venereal disease; severe menstrual cramps; allergy to copper; anemia; fainting attacks; unexplained genital bleeding or vaginal discharge; suspicious or abnormal Pap smear.

Long-term effect on ability to have children: Pelvic infection in some IUD users may result in their future inability to have children. Teenagers or women who would like to become pregnant in the future should probably use another method.

Diaphragm

A diaphragm is a shallow cup of thin rubber stretched over a flexible ring. A sperm-killing cream or jelly is put on both sides of the diaphragm, which is then placed by the woman inside the vagina before intercourse. The device covers the opening of the uterus, thus preventing the sperm from entering the uterus.

Effectiveness: Effectiveness depends on how correctly the method is used. Of 100 women who use the diaphragm with a spermicidal product for one year, 2 to 20 will become pregnant.

Advantages: No routine schedule to be kept as with The Pill. The diaphragm with a spermicidal product is inserted by the user.

No discomfort or cramping, as with the IUD. No effect on the chemical or physical processes of the body, as with The Pill or the IUD.

Disadvantages: Must be inserted before each intercourse and stay in place 6 to 8 hours afterwards.

Size and fit require yearly checkup, and should be checked if the woman gains or loses 15 pounds or more, has an abortion or gives birth.

The diaphragm requires instruction on insertion technique, which some women find difficult. The diaphragm must also be carefully maintained by washing, drying, and dusting it with cornstarch after each use (do not use talcum powder—it corrodes the rubber!).

Side Effects: The pressure of the diaphragm on the urethra may lead to urinary tract infections in some women. Allergic reactions to the rubber or spermicide may occur, but the problem is easily corrected.

Condom (Rubber)

The condom is a thin sheath of rubber or processed lamb cecum that fits over the penis.

Effectiveness: Effectiveness depends on how correctly the method is used. Of 100 women whose partner uses a condom for one year, 3 to 36 will become pregnant.

Advantages: In addition to contraception, the condom may afford some protection against venereal disease.

The condom is easily available, and requires no "long-term" planning before intercourse.

Disadvantages: Some people feel the condom reduces pleasure in the sex act. The male must interrupt foreplay and fit the condom in place before sexual entry into the woman. He must also quickly and carefully withdraw after orgasm.

The condom may slip or tear during use or spill during removal from the vagina.

Foam, Cream or Jelly alone (including suppositories)

Several brands of vaginal foam, cream or jelly can be used without a diaphragm. They form a chemical barrier at the opening of the uterus that prevents sperm from reaching an egg in the uterus; they also destroy sperm. In order to work effectively, the user must shake the can of foam well, and insert the foam deep in the vagina.

Effectiveness: Of 100 women who use aerosal foams alone for one year, 2 to 29 will become pregnant. Of 100 women who use jellies and creams alone for one year, 4 to 36 will become pregnant. No figures are available for suppositories, which are considered a fair to poor method of birth control. (If you do use suppositories, make sure they are specifically intended for birth control.)

Advantages: Easy to obtain, no prescription necessary.

Disadvantages: Must be used one hour or less before intercourse. If placed earlier, may become ineffective.

Side Effects: No serious side effects. Burning or irritation of the vagina or penis may occur. Allergic reactions may be corrected by changing brands.

Contraceptive Sponge

The contraceptive sponge is a round, disposable sponge saturated with spermicide which remains effective for 24 hours.

Effectiveness: Of 100 women who use the sponge for one year, 15 will become pregnant.

Advantages: Works for 24 hours, even for multiple acts of intercourse. No application of spermicide necessary, and is available without a prescription.

Disadvantages: Must stay in place at least six hours after intercourse.

Side Effects: The sponge caused a rash in 1.7 percent of women tested. There is no evidence yet that sponges cause Toxic Shock Syndrome, but doctors advise against their use during a woman's menstrual period.

Female Sterilization

Every year, about 700,000 women elect sterilization as their method of birth control. The primary method of sterilization for women is tubal sterilization, commonly referred to as "tying the tubes." A surgeon cuts, ties, or seals the fallopian tubes to prevent passage of eggs between the ovaries and the uterus. Several techniques are available, including one performed on an out-patient basis.

Effectiveness: Virtually 100 percent.

Advantages: A one-time procedure—never any more bother with devices or preparations of any kind.

Disadvantages: Surgery is required. Although in some cases a sterilization procedure has been reversed through surgery, the procedure should be considered permanent.

Side Effects: As with any surgery, occasionally there are complications, such as severe bleeding, infection or injury to organs which may require additional surgery to correct.

Long-term effect on ability to have children: When the traditional type of tubal ligation is used, it is reversible in some cases. However, ability to reverse should not be counted on.

Male Sterilization

Every year, about 500,000 men are sterilized in the U.S. Sterilization of men, called a vasectomy, involves severing the tubes through which the sperm travel. The procedure takes about half an hour and may be performed in a doctor's office under local anesthetic. A vasectomy does not affect a man's physical ability to have intercourse.

Effectiveness: Virtually 100 percent.

Advantages: A one-time procedure that does not require hospitalization and permits the man to resume normal activity almost immediately.

Disadvantages: The man is not sterile immediately after the operation—usually it takes a few months. Other means of contraception must be used during that time.

Side effects: Complications occur in 2 to 4 percent of cases, including infection, hematoma (trapped mass of clotted blood), granuloma (an inflammatory reaction to sperm that is absorbed by the body), and swelling and tenderness near the testes. Most such complications are minor and treatable without surgery.

Studies by the National Institutes of Health show that vasectomy does not affect a man's sexual desire or ability.

Long-term effect on ability to have children: Male sterilization is reversible in a fair number of cases, but ability to reverse should not be counted on.

"Natural Family Planning" (Rhythm method)

The woman must refrain from sexual intercourse on days surrounding the predicted time of monthly ovulation or, for greater effectiveness, until a few days after the predicted time of ovulation. The woman may use one of several methods to determine the time of ovulation by keeping records of menstrual periods, temperature, and the quality of cervical mucus.

Effectiveness: Of 100 women who use the calendar method for one year, 14 to 47 will become pregnant. Of 100 women who use the temperature method for one year, 1 to 20 will become pregnant. Of 100 women who use the mucus method for one year, 1 to 25 will become pregnant.

Women who take their temperature and also observe the changes in cervical mucus have a lower chance of pregnancy than if they used the calendar method alone. Out of 100 women, 1 in 22 will become pregnant.

Only 1 to 7 women out of 100 who have intercourse only after ovulation will become pregnant.

Advantages: No drugs or devices needed. Women will become more aware of their bodily processes.

Disadvantages: Requires careful recordkeeping and estimation of the time each month when there can be no intercourse.

To use any of the three methods properly a physician's guidance may be needed, at least at the outset.

If menstrual cycles are irregular, it is especially difficult to use this method effectively.

The couple may feel dissatisfied because of extended time each month when sexual intercourse must be avoided.

Side Effects: No physical effects, but because the couple must refrain from intercourse except on certain days of the month, using this method can create pressures on their relationship.

Withdrawal—Coitus Interruptus

This method of contraception requires withdrawal of the penis from the vagina before the man ejaculates, so the male sperm are not deposited at or near the birth canal. This method should not be considered effective in preventing pregnancy.

Douching

Use of a vaginal douche immediately after sexual intercourse to wash out or inactivate male sperm is not considered effective for preventing pregnancy.

Infertility

Half of the couples of childbearing age in the U.S. are physically unable to have children. 28 percent of the women have been surgically sterilized for contraceptive purposes, and another 11 percent for other medical reasons. Another 12 percent have some physical impairment which makes it difficult or impossible for the woman to carry a baby to term. Infertility among women has increased in the past twenty years probably because of more cases of pelvic inflammatory disease (PID). About 15 percent of the more than one million women affected by PID each year may become infertile. Researchers link the rise in PID with an increase in sexual activity at a younger age, intercourse with more partners, and a decreased use of barrier-method contraceptives, such as the diaphragm and condom, which can protect against PID.

An estimated 10 million men are impotent in the United States. Myron Murdock, the medical director of Impotents Anonymous, believes that in up to 85 percent of these cases, the problem is organic rather than psychological. Impotency can follow a stroke, spinal cord injuries and vascular diseases. Interestingly, the medications for these conditions can cause problems if combined with decongestants, sinus pills or tranquilizers. Cigarette and marijuana smoking, and drinking alcoholic beverages can cause impotency if combined with other drugs such as tranquilizers. Other causes include hardening of the arteries, radiation, and diabetes (an estimated 750,000 impotent men are diabetic). Arteriosclerosis, or hardening of the arteries, causes about half the cases of impotence in men over 50, although many men improve when they stop smoking and take drugs to dilate the arteries. If the causes of impotency cannot be otherwise cured, Murdock suggests the use of penile implants to restore sexual function.

In couples who would like to but are unable to have children, the infertility may be traced to the male in 30 to 40 percent of the cases. Along with the above-mentioned conditions, the production of sperm may be reduced by elevated scrotum temperatures, which can result from a hot bath, an infection, and even tight pants. Enlarged veins in the testes area is often the cause of male sterility, and can usually be treated with surgery requiring only an overnight hospital stay. Infection of the genital tract from a sexually transmitted disease may also cause infertility, and can often be treated with a tetracycline type antibiotic.

In some cases, a woman's infertility may be successfully treated with drugs. About half of all female infertility problems are due to infrequent or irregular ovulations; drug therapy can result in pregnancy in about a quarter of those women. Multiple births are a major side effect of these drugs: women who take Clomid, a common fertility drug, deliver more than one baby in 7 to 10 percent of the births, compared with a one percent multiple birth rate in the population as a whole (hence deserving of its nickname "Clone-id"). Women taking fertility drugs are more likely to have triplets, quadruplets and quintuplets than other women: multiple births of three or more babies make up only two percent of the whole population's births, opposed to 25% for women taking Clomid.

Some women do not require such powerful drugs, and may become pregnant after taking doses of a single hormone. In some cases, an overly acidic environment in the vagina may be killing off sperm, making a pre-intercourse douche with baking soda all that a women need do.

Notes
1. *Parade*, Lloyd Shearer, June 1984
2. *Human Sexuality*, Annette G. Godow, St. Louis, 1982

Chapter Six
Pregnancy

Happily, most pregnancies are safe and successful: 97.5 percent of all babies are born perfectly healthy. Of the small percentage of problem births, some are caused by genetic defects, while others could be prevented by proper nutrition and prudent habits. A look at the different factors that could affect your pregnancy follows.

 Drugs

Many of the changes the body goes through during pregnancy are accompanied by some degree of discomfort. Women accustomed to popping an aspirin for a headache or taking an antacid for an upset stomach may be surprised to learn that even these common practices could pose a risk to their baby. Almost every drug you take, from aspirin to antibiotics, passes through the placenta and reaches the fetus. Excessive aspirin use has been linked to mental retardation, limb abnormalities, fetal death, and bleeding in the newborn. Regular use of antacids may also increase the risk of birth defects. The antibiotic tetracycline can slow the baby's bone and teeth growth and cause discoloration of the child's teeth. To avoid exposing the fetus to hormones, women who become pregnant while using the Pill should stop taking it immediately and consult a physician. Women who go off the Pill in order to become pregnant should wait at least three months before attempting to conceive.

Always check with your obstetrician before taking any kind of medication. Specific information on the adverse effects of drugs can be found in the *Physicians' Desk Reference* available at the local library. Ideally, you should avoid *all* drugs during pregnancy. That doesn't mean that taking some medication during your pregnancy will definitely harm your baby. But the prudent rule to follow regarding any drug is unless it is prescribed by a doctor who knows you are pregnant, don't take it.

Caffeine, Alcohol and Tobacco

The Food and Drug Administration has cautioned pregnant women to avoid foods containing caffeine. Coffee, tea, cola and chocolate all contain caffeine. Studies have linked caffeine use with an increased risk of stillbirth, miscarriage and birth defects. Research reported in *Developmental Pharmacology and Therapeutics* suggests that pregnant women metabolize coffee more slowly than non-pregnant women, increasing the risk of toxic levels accumulating around the fetus.

Most doctors recommend pregnant women ingest no more than a moderate amount of caffeine, no more than one or two cups of coffee, tea or cola a day, if that much. As with aspirin, a little is probably safe, but none is even safer.

Will an occasional drink during pregnancy harm the baby? Researchers aren't sure; some evidence suggests that even small amounts of alcohol can contribute to poor growth in the fetus. Avoiding all alcohol is the most prudent advice. More conclusive research has found that pregnant women who drink one or more drinks a day give birth to smaller babies. Babies whose mothers drink heavily during pregnancy—three drinks or more a day—exhibit a pattern of birth defects known as Fetal Alcohol Syndrome, which causes growth deficiencies and heart defects, and is the third major cause of retardation in this country.

About 30 percent of pregnant women continue to smoke. Many women, while they have heard the general warning that "smoking is bad," do not understand how smoking will harm their child. The following risks are associated with smoking during pregnancy:

■ The risk of miscarriage is nearly three times greater for women smoking ten or more cigarettes a day than for nonsmokers.

■ The risk of premature birth is four times greater.

■ The risk of still birth is one and a half times greater.

■ Prenatal smoking is also linked to increased risk of birth defects such as hare lips and cleft palates, infant death and respiratory difficulties.

■ Children of smoking mothers are usually smaller at birth. If they grow up in a smoking household, these children may perform more poorly in school than children of nonsmokers, and are more likely to come down with colds, flu and pneumonia.

Infectious Diseases

Certain illnesses can be quite dangerous to the fetus if a mother develops them during pregnancy. A few simple precautions will prevent most problems.

German measles (rubella) can cause mental retardation, blindness, deafness, heart defects and death in the fetus. If you've had rubella, you won't get it again. If you're not sure, get a test for it before you get pregnant. If you're already pregnant, you will need to get frequent tests and must try to stay away from children to avoid infection. School-teachers and mothers of school-aged children obviously will have some difficulty here, making regular tests to check for exposure even more important.

Cats, and raw and very rare meat can be hosts for the parasite *Toxoplasma*. Infected infants may have mental retardation, poor brain development and eye defects. If you don't want to part with your cat, ask others to clean out the litter box, and have them wash their hands immediately afterward.

Other Precautions

■ Exercise helps the pregnant woman adjust to the physical, emotional and psychological changes of pregnancy. Women can continue to exercise throughout their pregnancies as long as they follow some simple guidelines. Work out aerobically for no more than 30 minutes at a time, and don't overdo it. Realize that you're not as coordinated or balanced and may not be able to maintain your pre-pregnancy pace. Swimming is an excellent sport for pregnant women because the water helps support additional weight.

■ Avoid unnecessary chemicals found in such products as artificial sweeteners and aerosol sprays. Don't put anything in your mouth without considering its safety.

■ X-rays of the head, neck, arms and legs probably do not affect the fetus, but every pregnant woman should inform the x-ray technician of her condition, and all nonessential x-rays should be avoided during pregnancy.

■ Sonography, or ultrasound, uses sound waves instead of x-rays to visualize the fetus. So far, no dangerous effects have been linked to ultrasound examinations, but as with all new techniques, it should not be used unless absolutely necessary.

■ Women who like soaking in hot tubs should be aware of a study at the University of Washington School of Medicine which found that a pregnant woman's internal temperature can rise to hazardous levels even after ten minutes in a hot tub. An excessive rise in temperature can damage the central nervous system of the fetus.

■ The safety of at-home births has been disputed by obstetricians, and nearly 99 percent of pregnant women in the U.S. still give birth in hospitals. Recent research by the Kentucky Department of Health Services found that women who plan on giving birth in the home or other non-hospital setting have no greater risk of problem deliveries than women in hospitals. Women interested in home birth should discuss their choice with their doctor. Most large cities have some kind of home birth service.

Tubal Pregnancies

Tubal, or ectopic, pregnancies, in which the fertilized egg develops outside the uterus, have reached epidemic proportions in the U.S. The number of ectopic pregnancies has tripled in the last 12 years. There are now about 15 ectopic pregnancies for every 1,000 live births.

In a typical ectopic pregnancy, the embryo grows inside the fallopian tube until the tube ruptures, causing internal bleeding which can be fatal. About 40 to 50 women die from ruptured ectopic pregnancies each year. Black women and women ages 35 to 44 have a higher risk of ectopic pregnancies.

Some physicians suspect that the rise in ectopic pregnancies is related to the increased number of pelvic infections in the last two decades. Women can reduce the risk of these infections by limiting the number of sexual partners and using barrier methods of contraception such as the diaphragm and condom.

Women should seek medical help *immediately* if they experience a delayed and spotty menstrual period, nausea, dizziness, and pain in the abdomen, shoulder, or diaphragm. Women who have had one ectopic pregnancy have a greater risk of having another. IUD's should not be used, as they increase the risk of infection. Induced abortions do not increase the risk of developing an ectopic pregnancy.

Miscarriage

Miscarriage ends about 15 to 20 percent of known pregnancies. The figure is probably higher because some miscarriages occur before the woman realizes she is pregnant, and a slightly delayed, heavy menstrual period is all she notices. In fact, about 75 percent of all miscarriages occur in the first three months.

The risk of miscarriage increases with age. Women under 25 with no previous history of miscarriage have about one chance in 400 of miscarrying. The risk roughly doubles for women in their early thirties, and doubles again for women in their late thirties.

Women who have had one miscarriage have a slightly increased risk of having another. At the same time, 80 percent of women who have previously miscarried are able to deliver a healthy baby. Women who have had three or more miscarriages, however, have much lower chances of carrying a baby to term.

The disappointment of miscarriage often leaves parents feeling guilty. Couples may worry that strenuous exercise or sexual intercourse caused the woman to miscarry, but it is nearly impossible to "traumatize" a healthy pregnancy in these ways. In the majority of miscarriages, the fetus is abnormal and cannot survive. While it is true that cigarette smoking, improper nutrition, certain drugs and environmental pollutants can increase the risk of miscarriage, the abnormality in the fetus is usually caused by a chance event and does not mean that there is anything wrong with the mother's egg or the father's sperm.

Chapter Seven

'Till Divorce Do Us Part:
Marriage and Divorce

The media often focuses attention on the runaway divorce rate and the decline of the family. Indeed, the divorce rate has increased steadily since 1960—today about half of all marriages end in divorce in the United States, although now it seems to be levelling off a bit. Overall, about 11.5 million people are divorced in the United States, about seven percent of the population aged 18 and over. That means, based on the 1984 unemployment rate, you're more likely to be out of a job than a spouse in modern America. If that fact does not console, it is also true that 1 in 8 marriages do make their "golden" anniversary of fifty years.

Attitudes about divorce are changing. In the past, it was widely assumed that divorce was an insurmountable political hurdle for a man in public life, a stigma that skewered the ambitions of Ireland's Charles Parnell in the last century and dashed the hopes for an American presidency of Adlai Stevenson and Nelson Rockefeller in modern times. Divorced women were often considered "tainted." Now, divorce has become more commonplace. It may well be that increased mobility and better communications have brought us into contact with more people and more divergent opinions than our forebears encountered, perhaps softening our once-strict censure of divorce.

Age of Dissent

With more than half of all women in the workforce, the traditional pattern of the stay-at-home mother and bread-winning father is shifting. But the strains of balancing a family and a career (still more of a woman's balancing act than a man's), the sexual revolution and the mobility of modern society all conspire to break young marriages. The divorce rate for women is highest for those aged 15 to 19, with the 20 to 24 age group a close second; for men, it is highest for those 20 to 24.[1] Of course we are not helpless to social tides. Personally we can reduce the "risk" of divorce by sensitizing ourselves to the effort necessary to make any marriage work.

Is the "seven year itch" responsible for so many parting couples? It is true that half of all divorces occur within the first seven years. The most treacherous single year seems to be the second. One sampling of over 500,000 divorces and annulments showed almost twice as many divorces after two years than after seven.

For both men and women, second marriages are more precarious than the first. First marriages last about seven years, while second marriages last an average of 4.5 years.[2]

Apparently, it is also true that the longer you're married, the longer you're likely to stay married, although there seems to be a rash of divorces between the fifth and ninth years of marriage. In the above mentioned sampling, the fewest number of divorces occurred in the group married 30 years or more, almost half the number, in fact, of those in the "honeymoon" group—couples married less than a year!

What are the major reasons marriages fail? One study of divorced couples listed the following:[3]

1. Infidelity
2. No longer loved each other
3. Emotional problems
3. Financial problems
4. Physical Abuse
5. Alcohol
6. Sexual problems
7. Problems with in-laws
8. Neglect of children
9. Communication problems
10. Married too young
11. Job conflicts

Of course, one must note that although a couple might pinpoint the final straw as infidelity, or problems with in-laws, these situations are usually symptoms of the deeper problem, often a lack of genuine communication and mutual respect.

The Cheating Heart

Between 50-60 percent of men, and 30-45 percent of women engage in an extramarital affair before age 40. Almost half of all working women have affairs, compared with only 25 percent of non-working wives, according to a survey taken by *Glamour* magazine. A survey of marriage counselors revealed that 85 percent of the counselors believed that marriages can recover if adultery occurs. Reinforcing the old double standard, more counselors believed that the wife's adultery would damage the marriage more than the husband's.

A study at Florida State University found that aggressive, "macho" men are no more likely to have affairs than "sympathetic and emotional" men. The same study indicated that monogamous men often still desire sexual variety, but fear disrupting their marriage. About two-fifths of the men surveyed who had affairs had a total of three to nine partners. Many of the adulterous men claimed that they loved their wives.

A 1977 survey of male attitudes about love, sex and women found that two-thirds of single men who lived with their girlfriends had cheated at least once, ten percent with their partner's knowledge and consent. Younger men were more likely to cheat than older ones. 72 percent of black males admitted to having cheated, as opposed to 47 percent of white males.

Portrait of an Adulterer/Adulteress

Some common characteristics:

■ They work as free-lancers, have jobs with flexible hours, and/or travel frequently.

■ Their verbal skills are high.

■ They married too young, and may feel wistful about not "playing the field" enough.

■ They have low self-esteem, look to the affair for a boost in self-confidence.

■ Their marriage is already in trouble, the affair is a way to avoid facing problems, an attempt to escape.

More Brains, More Dissatisfaction?
Education and Divorce

Do the years you've spent inside a classroom have any effect on your chances of seeing the inside of a divorce court? Of a sampling of over 300,000 divorces in 1978, more divorces (between 33 and 37 percent) occurred when both husband and wife had 12 years of schooling than at any other educational level. At both ends of the educational scale, the rates drop dramatically: at 17 or more years of school, only 4.8 percent of the men and 5 percent of the women were divorced, and at zero to eight years of school, only 6.9 percent of the husbands and 4.8 percent of the wives untied the knot. More than half of all women with graduate degrees who marry will divorce. Highly educated black women divorce more often than their white counterparts.

Where and Where Not

A United Nations study found the highest rate of divorce in Puerto Rico, at 3.35 per 1,000. The United States ranks second at 2.93, Sweden is twelfth at 1.42, Japan and Israel are tied for 27th at 0.87, Peru is 62nd at 0.15, and Mozambique, Angola and Guinea-Bissau are last, with no divorces recorded.

Urban areas where the migration rates are high often have high divorce rates.

More than one in three marriages in the Soviet Union end in divorce, according to a Russian sociologist, Yuri Ryurikov, who locates the trouble in unequally shared responsibilities between husband and wife. Russian wives usually work outside the home after marriage, but many husbands do not do their share of housework, child-rearing, and shopping.

Children

In an interview with a random sampling of 1,000 policyholders of a national insurance company, they found that a couple is more than twice as likely to contemplate divorce after the birth of children than before. Only ten percent of childless couples surveyed said they ever seriously considered separation or divorce, but that figure rises to 20 percent after the birth of a child. Stress was also found to peak when children are adolescents, while family closeness decreases.

Finding a Mate

■ It's Greenland for women and Reunion, a tiny French island in the Indian Ocean, for men. According to a United Nations study, 6 out of every 10 males in Greenland are available for matrimony. Two French islands in the Carribbean—Martinique and Guadeloupe—can also offer ample potential husbands. Men looking for wives might want to try Reunion, with almost 60 percent of the women available to marry.

■ If you fall in love with a colleague at the office, chances are 1 in 4 you will end up engaged or married, according to a *Glamour* magazine survey.

■ A woman's prospects for finding a husband decline as she gets older. A Princeton University study found the odds favoring white women aged 20-24, with 126 "suitable" white men for every 100 white

women. Black women in this age group have to look a little harder—
only 93 black men for every 100 black women.

The number of prospective grooms drops from age 25 on. For the
25-29 age group, 77 men to 100 women; 30-34 year olds, 62 men to 100
women. Women aged 60-64 have particularly slim pickings, with only
27 men to every 100 women. Why? Women live longer than men, and
remarrying older men often prefer to marry younger women. Older,
educated women have particular difficulty finding a compatible mate,
with only three suitable men available to every ten educated women.

■ Nonetheless, older unmarried women may at least have their
sanity. Married women make up the highest proportion of the mentally
ill, according to a Cornell University study. Marriage generally benefits
the mental health of men, but women often suffer more stress after
marrriage, as they may feel a loss of control over their lives.

Notes
1. National Center for Health Statistics Report, March 1985.
2. Redbook, March 1985.
3. *Journal of Marriage and the Family*, S.L. Albrecht, 1979

Chapter Eight
Hazards of Youth

Generally, we consider children more vulnerable to risk than adults. They are smaller and more fragile, with ferocious curiosities that exceed their common sense and coordination. An object harmless in the hands of an adult can become fatal in the hands of a child. Children *are* naturally protected against some risks which can be quite serious for adults. Their young, resilient bodies heal quickly: a fall on the ice which could fracture bones in an older person may cause only a bruise in a child.

While children do not yet have a long lifetime of bad habits threatening their health, the habits and attitudes they form during these years will affect their future well-being. Teaching children responsible habits early improves their odds against all risks.

Special Precautions for Young Kids

■ Tie knots in plastic bags, which can suffocate children, when disposing of them.

■ A partially filled mop bucket can be a hazard for toddlers. A study in *Clinical Pediatrics* investigated accidents in which nine- to twenty-month-old children fell into open buckets of liquid. Only a small percentage fully recovered; 62 percent died, and 15 percent were left retarded.

■ Childhood sunburns cause more than just temporary discomfort. Research at the New York University Medical Center suggests that several bad sunburns are more likely to cause a deadly form of skin cancer than chronic sun exposure. Have children use a sunscreen lotion which blocks out most of the sun's rays before playing outside, especially between the hours of 10 a.m. and 2 p.m.

■ What could be more innocent than baby powder? No baby powder. Some talcum powder is contaminated with asbestos. A recent study at Brigham and Women's Hospital in Boston has linked ovarian cancer with the practice of using talcum powder in and around the genital area. Use corn starch instead. (It's cheaper, too.)

■ Children between one and three years are most likely to inhale and choke on food. Some foods are more dangerous than others: candy, nuts, popcorn, hotdogs—any food small, round, hard or slippery which is difficult for a child to hold in place and chew may cause choking. Peanut butter spread too thickly on bread or given on a spoon can also be dangerous. To prevent choking, always have child eat while sitting upright. Avoid using anesthetic gels on babies gums before feeding time which numb the mouth and may make swallowing difficult.

■ Obtain "tot-finder" decals from the local fire department to identify your child's bedroom.

■ Teach children to never run with anything sharp in their hands or mouths.

■ Remove control knobs on the stove if possible, replacing them when you need to cook.

■ Add dishwasher detergent to the dishwasher only when you are ready to start it. The cups filled with colored powder on an open door may attract curious toddlers.

■ Discourage eating in the car. It's hard to respond to a choking child while driving.

Toying with Risk

Children will invariably use toys in ways a parent might not ever dream of, turning what would appear to be a harmless plaything into a deadly device. The Consumer Product Safety Commission reports a drop in toy-related deaths, but still believes the numbers are too high. In 1983, for example, 16 children died, and 118,000 others were injured by toys.

Toys to watch out for:

■ Half of the children who died in toy-related deaths in 1983 choked or swallowed small toys, parts of toys or balloons. Balloons can be particularly dangerous—children who put uninflated balloons or small pieces of burst balloons in their mouths may choke or suffocate. More than 80 small children have died in such a manner over the last 10 years.

■ Rattle and squeeze toys have caused 18 deaths and 106 choking incidents in which the toy became lodged in the infants' throats. The Safety Commission cautions that any squeeze toy smaller than the child's fist could cause choking.

■ Crib gyms should only be used for small infants, under five months. Older babies can get their hands, feet or clothing entangled in the dangling parts of the crib gym.

- The lids of toy chests have been known to fall on a child's head or neck, and have caused 21 deaths and two cases of permanent brain damage since 1973.
- Any toy with small parts, long strings or cords which can cause strangulation, or sharp edges or points is potentially dangerous.
- Toy guns that fire darts, corks or plastic cause nearly 1,000 injuries among children annually, many of them eye injuries to children under five years old.

Poisoning

Over 2.3 million people are poisoned annually in the United States, the victims predominantly children under 6. Fortunately, with prompt medical care most survive with little or no lasting physical effects; about 3,400 do not survive, however.

Most people know the importance of storing dangerous products safely out of children's reach, but many poisoning accidents occur when the product is in use. You may be cleaning the floor or varnishing a chair, the phone rings and you leave for just a moment—enough time for your curious child to wander in and take a swallow. Remember also that little hands love to rummage through pockets and purses—you may have locks on your cabinets, but forget that your handbag holds aspirin or perfume. Children drinking perfume or mouthwash can be poisoned by the alcohol they contain—in one case, a child entered a coma after drinking half a bottle of mouthwash. Of course, sampling the real stuff can also lead to alcohol poisoning, as happened to one little girl who sipped drinks set out at her parent's cocktail party.

Peak poisoning times are about 10-11 o'clock in the morning and 4-6 o'clock in the evening, perhaps because children are less supervised during these times, and may be hungry or restless. Children will put anything in their mouths. They can mistake roach powder or boric acid for sugar or flour; they may chew on a houseplant leaf which is toxic; they may sample a mothball, only to gasp at its bad taste and then choke on the ball.

Aspirin and aspirin-type drugs cause one-third of all fatal drug poisonings. Sedatives, hypnotics, barbituates and heart drugs follow in frequency. Camphorated oil is sometimes mistaken for cod-liver oil and causes about 500 poisonings a year. People have also been poisoned by utensils which have not been thoroughly washed after cleaning with silver polish.

Always follow directions for taking medications. Never transfer medicine from its original container to another. This practice can only invite confusion. Never take medicine in the dark. Do not keep medicine after the illness for which it was prescribed has ended.

Many common indoor and outdoor plants are poisonous if chewed, swallowed or rubbed against the skin. The homey philodendron is one of the most frequently ingested poisonous plants. The Dumbcane, or Dieffenbachia, gets its name from the crystals of calcium oxalate in its stalk that can swell the tongue enough to block the air passage with possibly fatal results. Nausea, vomiting, diarrhea, and even death are the unpleasant possibilities awaiting a victim who eats a few mistletoe berries, the leaves of rhubarb, tomatoe, or foxglove. Azaleas, daffodils, and autumn crocus bulbs are also poisonous. Rosary pea seeds, with their attractive red and black enamel shells, are often made into necklaces. A single seed can kill a child.

To prevent poisoning tragedies, keep small children away from dangerous plants, and teach older ones never to put any plant or berry in their mouths not used as a food. Keep all cleaning products, insecticides or other dangerous chemicals in places inaccessible to children. Be extra observant when actually using a household product, especially the very caustic ones such as toilet bowl or drain cleaner. If you must leave the room for the phone, even if just for a moment, take the product or your child with you. Never put any poisonous product in a container which once held food. Your local poison control center may offer special poison warning labels which can help prevent a needless accident. Don't tell children any medicine is like "candy" or delicious, and try not to take medicines in front of children, as they are great imitators. Avoid storing cleaning products on the same shelves as food, and buying scented cleaning products which may be more appealing to children.

Keep de-icer spray locked in the trunk. Just a little in the eyes can cause blindness.

Label potentially poisonous items with "Mr. Yuk" stickers (Mr. Yuk, above) is available from:

National Capital Poison Center
Georgetown University Hospital
3800 Reservoir Road, N.W.
Washington, D.C. 20007

Teach your children that Mr. Yuk means "don't touch!" Also alert them about dangerous items which cannot be labeled easily, such as cigarette butts and some cosmetics.

List of Products to Label:

Kitchen
•vitamins
•drain cleaners
•furniture polish
•pet medicine
•all cleaners
•insecticides, rat poisons

Garage
•lime and fertilizer
•paints and varnishes
•turpentine, kerosene
•gasoline
•antifreeze
•weed killers

Other Items
•cigarettes, cigars, butts
•felt tip markers
•flaking paint
•insulation

Bathroom
•soaps and shampoos
•detergents
•deodorizers
•mouthwash
•aftershave and cologne
•suntan lotion
•medicine
•deodorants

Bedroom
•medicines
•cosmetics
•nail polish and remover

Lead Poisoning

Once associated only with children living in slums, lead poisoning is now recognized as a hazard which does not discriminate between the various geographic and socioeconomic groups. The Centers for Disease Control recently found that lead can be toxic at levels lower than recently thought, and that four out of every 100 children under age 5 have enough lead in their blood to cause adverse effects. Low levels of lead cause learning disabilities such as impaired verbal ability and shortened attention span, and behavioral problems such as hyperactivity, clumsiness, or frequent mood swings. Comas, convulsions and even death can result from exposure to high levels of lead.

How are we exposed to lead?

Lead-based paint covers the walls of about 40 million housing units in the U.S. which were built before 1940. While less than a half milligram of lead is considered a safe daily intake, a tiny flake of lead-based paint can contain 100 milligrams of lead.

Exhaust from cars and trucks emits lead which can settle into dust and soil, and even contaminate animals grazing nearby.Urban children should never eat snow, which can absorb lead from the air, nor icicles, which can contain more concentrated amounts of lead.

The practice of burning old batteries for heat by poor families has caused many severe cases of lead poisoning.

How are children at risk?

Children absorb lead more readily than adults, and more of the lead they do absorb affects the soft tissues of the bone marrow, kidney and brain. Children between 9 months and 6 years are particularly at risk, as they tend to put more things in their mouths. In addition, if the child's diet is low in iron, protein or calcium, the body absorbs an increased amount of lead.

Early signs of lead poisoning include fatigue, insomnia, headaches and muscle pains. However, one disturbing finding of a 1971 study of Philadelphia schoolchildren was that about 20 percent of the children who had elevated lead levels *showed no symptoms.* The Centers for Disease Control recommends that every child in the United States be tested for lead poisoning.

You can take measures at home to reduce the incidence oflead poisoning in children. A study at Sinai Hospital in Baltimore found that families who wet-mopped floors and washed children's hands regularly caused the lead levels in the children's blood to drop dramatically.

Vaccines

Some health specialists worry that the absence of epidemics thanks to vaccinations have given parents a false sense of security which is preventing them from having their children inoculated against disease. Most new parents, vaccinated themselves as children, have no firsthand knowledge of such frightening illnesses as polio, whooping cough and smallpox, and consider them ailments of the past. In addition, debates over the safety of vaccines have entered the public arena. Parents who said their children had suffered neurological problems after receiving vaccinations have spoken out on television talk shows and in magazine articles. What are the facts?

In 1932, one of every 12 children died before age five, mostly from diseases such as whooping cough, measles, diptheria and tetanus. Today these diseases are rare. Now, only one child in 650 dies before age five, with most deaths caused by accidents, birth defects and premature births rather than infectious diseases.

British children found themselves guinea pigs in a living experiment in 1978 after an article in a British medical journal reported that a small number of children suffered adverse reactions to immunization against

81

whooping cough (pertussis). As fearful parents began to refuse to have their children immunized, the number of whooping cough cases sky-rocketed, reaching epidemic proportions. A worried British government commissioned a national study, which concluded that neurological reactions to pertussis vaccines were very rare, about one in every 110,000 doses, and that the chance of a child suffering any lasting damage was 3.2 in a million.

Doctors advise that children should *not* be immunized if:

- they are sick the day the immunization is scheduled.
- they suffer from seizures or any progressive neurological disorder.
- they reacted to an earlier immunization with convulsions, collapse, or encephalitis.

Parents should consult their physician if a child reacts to an immunization with excessive fatigue, screaming or high temperature.

Not for Adults Only

Stress

The aggressive "Type A" behavior which can contribute to high blood pressure and heart disease in the middle-aged is not acquired overnight (see Chapter One). Researchers are finding that the harmful personality traits of intense competitiveness, impatience, and easily aroused hostility emerge in children as young as three to six years old. Although the children's drive to achieve can also contribute to their success in academics and sports, their behavior changes the way their bodies respond to the stresses of everyday life, and can cause trouble in later years. Compared to their more relaxed "Type B" peers, Type A children have higher heart rates and blood pressure.

Dr. Meyer Friedman, who first coined the term "Type A" behavior, suggest that parents be alert to the warning signs of Type A traits, such as:

- difficulty showing affection to parents or siblings;
- crying or throwing a temper tantrum after losing a game or playing a sport;
- physical signs of restlessness or impatience: knee jiggling, finger tapping, interrupting conversations;
- attempts to do many things at once.[1]

Friedman suggests that parents learn to love their children unconditionally, as well as becoming aware of how they handle their own anger, which the child is likely to imitate. Pushing the child too hard to achieve can be a big mistake. A study recently presented to the American Association of School Administrators has found that children who enter kindergarten when they are only four years old are much more likely to fail in later grades than their older classmates. Among the younger students, 23 percent had failed a grade, compared with only 7 percent of the older group.

Diet and Exercise

We may not acquire a taste for okra or creamed herring until adulthood, but the habits of sweetening, salting and buttering food start early. A 14 year study of 8,000 children in Bogalusa, Louisiana, has found that fatty deposits in the arteries can begin to develop in childhood, especially in heavy children who eat a lot of fatty foods. Children who eat a lot of salty foods are more likely to have high blood pressure *while they are children,* not just later in life. The study found that boys, especially black boys, ate more salty foods and had higher blood pressures than girls. Black girls in the study exercised the least and were most likely to be overweight.

Do your children a favor and encourage them to adopt healthful eating and exercising habits. Don't let them get hooked on salt, sugar, or junk food. Substitute low-salt crackers, homemade popcorn, fruit, and vegetable sticks for potatoe chips, pretzels and cookies. Don't use sweets as a reward. Set an example and quit smoking if you do, exercise regularly, and improve your diet.

Teenage Suicide

In the last few years, teenage suicide has made a lot of headlines. This section will look at the figures available, note the signs commonly associated with the suicidal individual, and suggest ways to help, while recognizing that this "risk" defies simple definition and hence simple prevention.

The disturbing facts:

■ Every 90 minutes, a teenager kills himself in the U.S.

■ Every day, 1,000 young people will attempt suicide.

■ The teenage suicide rate has tripled since the 1950's. In 1983, at least 6,000 youths took their own lives. Since suicides may be reported as accidents, the figure is probably much higher. One estimate figures that for every reported suicide, another 15-30 go unreported, putting the 1983 figure somewhere between 6,000 and 180,000 teenage suicides.

■ 90 percent of all suicide attempts are made by females, but males succeed more often. Males generally use more violent means to end their lives, such as shooting or hanging themselves, which makes the possibility of intervention and rescue less likely. Females are more likely to try less effective methods such as taking drugs.

- Suicide pacts and "cluster" suicides in which several suicides occur in the same area over a short time, appear to be a new phenomenon.

Portrait of the suicidal teenager—a thousand faces

Although suicidal individuals share some common characteristics, they may express their distress in different ways and to varying degrees.

Some common causes of suicide:

- low self esteem;
- feelings of helplessness or inability to overcome problems;
- pressures from school, parents, peers;
- loneliness, feelings of abandonment, loss;

Signs to be aware of:

- depression;
- change in eating or sleeping habits;
- drug or alcohol abuse;
- headaches, fears of illness, decreased sex drive;
- talking about suicide, excessive feelings of guilt, beliefs that others will be better off without the person;
- withdrawal from friends, family, activities; a listless attitude.

What to do:

- Listen to the person. Take his or her feelings seriously.
- Do not say "Oh, don't be silly, everything will be fine." Acknowledge the person's depression, and let him or her know others do care and help is available.
- A teacher, counselor or clergyman can be of service, as can a suicide prevention hotline or community mental health counseling service.

Teen Suicide Rates for Selected Countries

Ages 15-24 years; rate per 100,000 population

Country	Males	Females
Australia	17.6	4.5
Austria	30.1	10.5
Canada	27.8	5.7
Denmark	17.3	5.1
France	14.0	5.2
Germany, Fed. Rep.	21.2	6.4
Ireland	6.2	2.5
Israel	10.8	1.2
Japan	16.6	8.2
Netherlands	5.3	3.8
Norway	20.2	3.3

Poland	19.5	4.3
Sweden	16.9	5.8
Switzerland	34.8	12.5
United Kingdom	7.0	2.1
United States	20.2	4.3

Source: World Health Organization, 1981 figures

Notes
1."Type A Tots" by Sally Squires, *Washington Post,* February 20, 1985

Chapter Nine
Risky Businesses:
Your Chances as an Entrepreneur

What is your chance of making a big killing in business or of going bankrupt? Of course the risks depend on your skills, but also on where the business is located, and on the type of business selected. As I do not know your individual skills I can only give statistical chances for the average business of a certain type.

Most of the data clearly shows that the risk of failure is lowest when you buy a franchise from an established company. The results of surveys have indicated that more than half of all new consumer products introduced by large companies fail. If these major corporations, with large advertising and research budgets, fail, the chances of a new company introducing a new product must be even less. However, many innovative products have come from small companies, such as the pet rock, the Trivial Pursuit board game and the Apple personal computer.

Franchising Facts

While the risks of buying a business from a major franchisor is less risky than starting your own similar business, the price of buying a franchise eliminates many small investors. The typical McDonald's franchise takes $140,000 in non-borrowed funds, and financing for about $200,000 in additional funding. A Midas Muffler franchise requires a $150,000 commitment of funds, most of which can be borrowed. Baskin-Robbins ice cream stores require an investment of between $25,000 and $50,000. The types of businesses available via franchise vary widely from car dealerships, to hotel chains, including Holiday Inns and Sheraton Inns, donut shops to Hertz and Avis car rentals.

If you are interested in obtaining a list of available franchises you should obtain a copy of *Franchise Opportunities Handbook* , U.S. Department of Commerce, from the Government Printing Office or a library. This book contains detailed information on nearly 2,000 franchisors and includes background information about this type of business investment.

About one out of 30 franchisee-owned businesses discontinued operation during 1983. The risks of particular franchises is difficult to assess because if a McDonalds or a Burger King is in trouble, the franchisor will often quietly buy out the investors. The major risk with a well-known franchise is picking the right location.

In 1983 there were 355,392 franchisee-owned outlets in the United States. Excluding car dealerships, gas stations and soft drink bottlers, there were 194,335 franchises. Of these just under seven thousand discontinued business in that year, or about 3.5%.

The following table demonstrates that different types of franchises have wide ranges of risks:

Type of Franchise	Discontinuance Rate (1983)
Recreation, entertainment travel	2.3%
Restaurants	2.4%
Educational products and services	2.4%
Food retailing (other than convenience stores	2.4%
Auto/truck rental	2.9%
Construction, home improvement, maintenance & cleaning	3.1
Automotive products & services	3.3%
Hotels, motels & campgrounds	3.4%
Retailing (non-food)	3.6%
Convenience stores	3.8%
Laundry & dry cleaning	3.9%
Business aids & services (includes accounting, real estate, tax preparation and printing services)	4.2%
Equipment rental	6.0%

Although franchising is predominantly an American phenomenon, franchising is spreading throughout the world. In 1983, 305 U.S. franchising companies had opened more than 25,000 franchises in foreign countries. Since 1973 the number of U.S. franchisors operating overseas has doubled, and the number of their foreign outlets has increased eight-fold.

U.S. Franchises Overseas

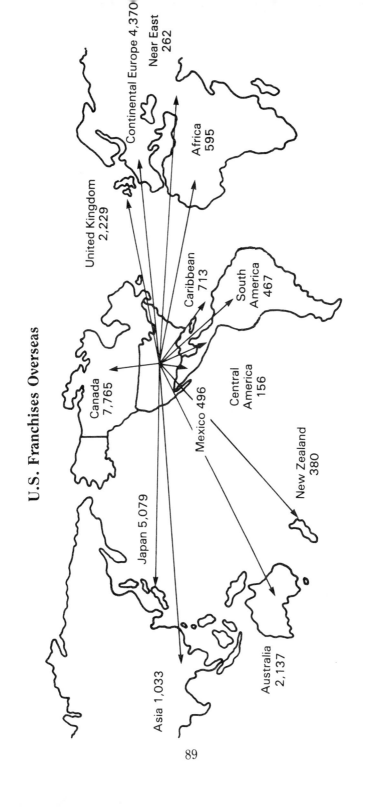

Continental Europe 4,370

Near East 262

Africa 595

United Kingdom 2,229

Caribbean 713

South America 467

Canada 7,765

Central America 156

Mexico 496

New Zealand 380

Japan 5,079

Asia 1,033

Australia 2,137

When and Why Businesses Fail

Slightly more than half of business failures in the United States occur during the first five years of operation. Since 1976 the range of this statistic has been between 53 and 54%. The following chart shows when businesses fail:

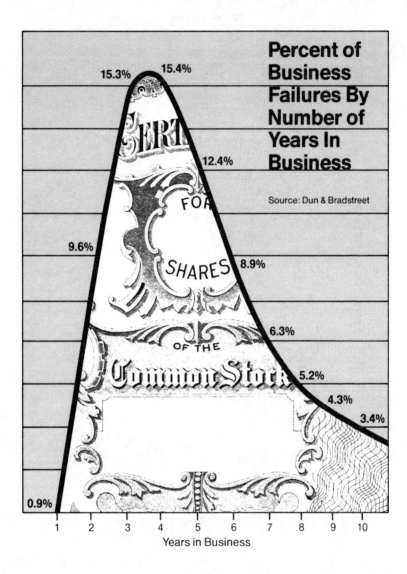

Percent of Business Failures By Number of Years In Business

Source: Dun & Bradstreet

15.3%   15.4%

12.4%

9.6%

8.9%

6.3%

5.2%

4.3%

3.4%

0.9%

1 2 3 4 5 6 7 8 9 10

Years in Business

Managerial inexperience or incompetence is the cause of 95% of business failures. This includes lack of experience in the line of business entered (14.9%), lack of managerial experience (16.1%), unbalanced experience (lacking experience in sales, finance, purchasing or production (19.7%)), and incompetence (44.1%). The result of this managerial inexperience or incompetence resulted in inadequate sales nearly 60% of the time, and excessive operating expenses nearly 30% of the time. In other cases the result was difficulty collecting receivables or competitive weakness. Many failing businesses experienced more than one of these resulting difficulties.

Business Failures by State

The only statistics available are for business bankruptcies. A business can fail even though it doesn't file for bankruptcy. However, business bankruptcies, by region, and by type of business provide a reasonable relationship with business risks. Comparisons from state to state are valid, as are comparisons from one type of business to another, since the same statistics are available for all regions and all businesses.

For 1980 Wyoming had the least business bankruptcies per 10,000 businesses while Washington State had the most:

State*	Bankruptcies per 10,000 businesses
Wyoming	2.6
Arizona	6.3
Vermont	7.1
New Hampshire	11.9
Rhode Island	13.7
Utah	15.7
Missouri	22.1
Florida	24.7
West Virginia	24.8
New York	28.8
Connecticut	29.5
Iowa	29.5
Louisiana	31.9
Colorado	33.0
North Carolina	34.2
Delaware	36.4
Massachusetts	37.0
Maryland	37.2
New Mexico	37.2

State	Bankruptcies per 10,000 businesses
Arkansas	38.8
Mississippi	38.8
Wisconsin	39.1
Nevada	40.5
Indiana	43.5
Ohio	44.4
Alabama	45.2
Maine	45.6
Georgia	45.7
Kentucky	46.3
Idaho	49.5
Pennsylvania	50.2
Kansas	51.8
Virginia	52.3
New Jersey	53.6
Nebraska	57.5
Illinois	58.0
Oklahoma	69.0
North Dakota	70.0
California	70.0
South Dakota	74.5
Michigan	76.3
Montana	79.3
Oregon	85.9
Tennessee	101.1
Washington	177.8

* Alaska, D.C., South Carolina and Hawaii deleted because of incomplete data; Source: Dun & Bradstreet.

Types of Businesses and their Riskiness

Failure rates in different industries can provide valuable information to potential investors. However, the data often lags years behind. For example, the hot industries of the last few years, computers, video rentals and video games, can turn cold before the initial data is ever published. Later on we will discuss risks of entering business as a franchisee as compared to an independent business. Dun and Bradstreet data on the failure rates in various retail businesses: [failure rates show bankrupcies, but do not include businesses which disappeared without filing for bankruptcy]

Retail Business Failures

Lines of business	Failure rate per 10,000
Infants and children's wear	58
Furniture and furnishings	56
Sporting goods	56
Women's ready-to-wear clothing	53
Cameras and photo supplies	49
Men's wear	48
Appliances, radio and TV	44
Lumber & building materials	36
Automobiles	36
Auto parts & accessories	33
Carpet and fabric	31
Shoes	29
Restaurants and bars	26
Books & stationery	25
Gift	23
Toys & crafts	22
Bakeries	19
Jewelry	16
Grocery, meat & produce	15
Drugs	13
Department stores	11
Women's accessories	9

Failures in Manufacturing Businesses

Furniture	105
Transportation equipment	102
Textiles	79
Leather and shoes	61
Apparel	58
Electrical machinery	52
Rubber & plastic products	45
Metals, primary and fabricated	43
Lumber	38
Chemicals and drugs	36
Printing and publishing	34
Stone, clay and glass	33
Machinery except electrical	33
Food	29
Paper	29

The Risks of Inventions

If you have an idea for a new product which is patentable, your odds of making $100,000 or more profit from it are about 1 in 1,500. About 80,000 patents are issued annually in the United States. Only about 50 of those involve patents by individuals who turn the patent into a small fortune. Most of the patents are issued to large corporations.

So You Want to Write a Movie!

Just 14,000 screenplays are registered with the Writers Guild of America annually. Thousands more are written but not registered with the Guild. There are between 300 and 400 movies made each year. Your chances of turning your screenplay into a movie are about 1% or less, depending on your Hollywood connections.

Books

In the United States there are about 40,000 new books published each year, and about 150 could be considered "best sellers". If your book makes the best-seller list it could earn you from $25,000 to $1 million or more. If your book is published your chances of it making the best seller list are about one in 250. Your chances of getting a book published are higher than that. However most of the 40,000 books are published by established authors (authors of previous books or magazine articles or newspaper reporters). Your chances of getting your book published increase dramatically if you are able to find a literary agent willing to present your book to publishers.

Conclusion

Well, you knew that starting a business was risky. But you want to start your own business anyway. You don't want to open a fast-food franchise. What you should look for are niches. And you have to rely on your gut feelings. If you know an area well and believe that "this place needs a bagel bakery," then investigate the bagel business and go for it. If you believe in a product, and have done your homework investigating its potential, you have to take risks in order to succeed. Most successful writers, inventors and businessmen took great risks to develop businesses and products. If it weren't for risks taken in the past we would not have the telephone, computer or the light bulb.

Chapter Ten

Sports Risks

The fitness boom of the last several years leaves little doubt about the value of exercise. Prescribed to strengthen weak hearts, dissolve excess weight, clear the skin and calm the mind, exercise, coupled with sound nutrition, comes close to a true panacea.

As people age, many worry that they will "break their necks" or strain their hearts during physical exertion. If you are over 35 years old, and either overweight, a smoker, under a lot of stress, have high blood pressure, high cholesterol levels, or a family history of heart disease, or diabetes, then you should see a physician before beginning an exercise program. The odds of a middle aged man with *no* symptoms dying of heart failure during a vigorous workout are only one in five million. For women, the odds are only one in 17 million. Once the blood vessels become clogged with cholesterol, *excessive* activity can overwork the heart, but an exercise program promoting moderate exertion definitely outweighs sitting still.

The risk of many sports injuries can be reduced through proper training and equipment. Whatever sport you participate in, and regardless of your level of involvement, the cardinal rule is to know your sport. Don't assume that your single game of tennis a week exempts you from learning about the risks of various court surfaces; your knees could make you regret it. Learn what your sport demands of the body and how you can meet those demands without injury.

Insufficient conditioning and "overdoing it" are responsible for the majority of sports injuries of flabby beginner and seasoned athlete alike. The veteran runner with muscle-rippled legs can be courting a knee injury if he does nothing but run, albeit ten miles a day, and neglects strengthening the muscles which support the knee. Aerobic activity, which increases the body's capacity to use oxygen, has been hailed as the ticket to a healthy heart and lungs. But the recent "aerobic mania" should not lead athletes to neglect flexibility conditioning, which helps protect muscles from injury. Many athletes, impatient to get on with their game, do a few token stretches, if any. But cold, tight muscles are vulnerable muscles. A warm-up which raises body temperature and increases blood flow to the muscles improves flexibility and protects against injury.

The American College of Sports Medicine recommends an exercise routine involving limbering up with an easy jog in place, followed by about ten minutes of stretching exercises before beginning athletic activity. The warm-up should proceed slowly at first, and work up to a more vigorous pace. Athletes should end their workout by slowing down their pace and cooling down with slow stretching exercises. The cool-down helps prevent light headedness and fainting, and relaxes muscles, making them less vulnerable to injury. The worst thing you can do after vigorous exercise is to stop suddenly. A recent study conducted by Dr. Joel Dimsdale of Massachusetts General Hospital, found a "striking" increase in the levels of hormones that can produce irregular heartbeat in men who stopped suddenly after exercising vigorously. This heartbeat irregularity can be fatal to someone with an unhealthy heart. The lesson is not to stop exercising, but to cool down gradually before sitting or lying down. A good way to cool down is just to slow down the pace of whatever exercise you're doing—for example, walking for a few minutes after jogging.

The wise athlete also knows when to quit. A fatigued or overheated body loses coordination and strength, and to push oneself in this state is asking for sprains, pulls and tears. In contact sports, compete against others of comparable height and weight. Learn to listen to your body and work gradually to extend your limits, or you risk losing more time waiting for injuries to heal.

Preventing Common Sports Injuries

■ Considering 75 percent of all sports injuries occur during the first two weeks of the season, make sure you are in proper condition.

■ Blisters may be avoided by applying Vaseline to sensitive spots and wearing a thin pair of socks under a thicker pair.

■ Don't wear jewelry when playing any sport. Fingers have had to be amputated when the ring caught on some immovable object. One man lost a finger when his ring caught on the rim of a basketball net.

■ No, your voice won't change, and although they're mighty painful, serious groin injuries are very rare. Wear a jock strap when playing any sport.

Preventing Heat Injury

Working out in temperatures over 60 degrees may cause dehydration, heat exhaustion, or heat stroke. Beginners are especially at risk, as are the elderly, small children, and those who are overweight, whose hearts are weaker than more experienced athletes. In heat exhaustion, the brain does not get enough blood, and can lead to the more serious heat stroke if not treated properly. The victim of heat exhaustion can become dizzy, nauseous, and chilled while sweating profusely. Heat stroke interferes with the body's ability to cool itself—the victim stops sweating, has a high fever and may be dazed or unconscious. Immediate medical attention is necessary.

To reduce risk of heat injury:

■ Wear a hat and light colored clothing.

■ Exercise in early morning or evening, avoiding midday heat when sun is strongest.

■ Acclimitize gradually to heat by working out ten minutes one day, fifteen the next. Build up slowly, especially if you expect to compete on a hot day. Your body will "learn" to start sweating sooner.

■ Avoid strenuous exercise when the humidity is high, as the humidity slows the evaporation of sweat which cools the body.

■ Drink water before and during exercise. Avoid sugary or fruit drinks, as the glucose retards water absorption into the circulation. *Do not* replace lost fluids with alcoholic beverages. Alcohol generates heat in the body and throws off the heat control mechanism.

Risks of winter sports

Winter sports can harbor extra risks because people are generally less fit in the winter than they are in warmer months. Begin an exercise program which includes a cardiovascular workout, such as swimming, biking, or jogging, as well as strengthening exercises (such as weight lifting) and flexibility exercises, and do it *before* you take a week long ski holiday. Be sure to warm up slowly and rhythmically right before going out on the slopes or ice rink.

Another winter sport risk, which is the leading cause of death among winter backpackers and mountaineers, is hypothermia, a dangerous drop in body temperature as heat is lost faster than the body can produce it. You can suffer hypothermia if you *overdress* for the weather as well as underdress, as extra layers will make you sweat more and then trap perspiration close to the skin where it can chill the body. A moderately paced jog will generate a 25 to 30 degree temperature increase, so if it's 30 degrees out, choose clothing which would keep you warm on a 55 to 60 degree day. A plethora of high-tech materials such as Gore-Tex, polypropylene and Lycra are now used to make foul weather clothing for athletes that insulates the body and allows perspiration to pass out away from the skin. Outfitting yourself in these latest items can get quite expensive. Instead, you can dress in layers, avoiding cotton next to the skin, which traps sweat. You may want to invest in polypropylene bodywear, about $17 each for pants and top, at this writing.

Frostbite: Frostbite occurs when the body tries to conserve heat in the vital organs by reducing circulation to the extremities. The skin and underlying tissues freeze; blood flow stops in the affected area and ice crystals form between cells.

 ■ Keep a layer of warm air near the skin by dressing in layers. Keep extra mittens and socks on hand in case your other pairs get wet.

 ■ Make sure you're well-fed, and carry high-energy foods, such as raisins and nuts.

 ■ Be aware that alcohol dilates the blood vessels and allows more blood to become chilled. Tobacco constricts the blood vessels, reducing the warming effects of circulation.

 ■ Avoid wearing metal framed eyeglasses which can freeze to the skin, or touching any metal, such as on cameras.

 ■ Male runners have been known to suffer from the not very pleasant frostbite of the penis on cold days. Wear extra covering, or buy special insulated underpants at a sporting goods store.

Thunderstorms can be dangerous to anyone, but are particularly threatening to golfers and bicyclists. Most lightening deaths occur in open fields, such as golf courses and ball parks. Lightening storms cause about 100 deaths and 245 injuries each year. You have a one in 2,000,000 chance of dying from being struck by lightening. To avoid tragedy during a storm:

 ■ Golfers should get off their carts and put down their clubs immediately. Stand in a low place; don't lie on the ground.

 ■ Stay away from hills and open water.

 ■ Stay away from fences and other metal objects.

 ■ Get off tractors and other farm equipment.

- Avoid standing in small isolated structures.
- Seek shelter under a thick growth of small trees in a wooded area.
- If you are standing in an open field and your hair stands on end, a storm is coming.

Running

The running movement in America, which peaked in the seventies, has subsided today only to the degree that fewer beginners are hitting the pavement, while "seeded," committed runners have secured the movement as a national institution. Running's virtues, from the "runner's high" to its aerobic benefits, are as well-known as its purported dangers, which range from shin splints to loss of calcium in the bones. Runners should remember that their sport threatens more musculoskeletal injuries—damage to bones, muscles, and fibrous tissues—than all other sports combined. These risks can be reduced by learning to anticipate where and how you may be vulnerable to injury, and making the necessary compensations.

Risks of Running

Musculoskeletal injuries

More than a third of runners in a recent Journal of the American Medical Association survey suffered a musculoskeletal injury severe enough to force them to decrease their weekly mileage.

The risk of injury increases as weekly mileage increases. A sudden increase in mileage or speed before your muscles are adequately strengthened invites muscle pulls and tendon strains. Whether you are a devoted runner upping your mileage from four to six miles a day, or a novice with a yen to run around the block after years of inactivity, you must *gradually* strengthen your muscles to meet the new demand. My own running career came to a halt after I ran five miles more than I was used to, and then continued to run with a pain in my knee until I could hardly walk. Had I taken an extra ten minutes a day to strengthen my leg muscles, and, more importantly, listened when my knees cried for me to ease up, I could have avoided a lot of unnecessary pain and frustration.

To prevent running injuries:
- Wear shoes with proper fit and support. Some runners report that a stubborn ache disappears with a new pair of shoes. Knee pains are often linked to problems in the foot. A podiatrist may suggest special shoe inserts.

- Proper running style: feet should strike ground directly below body, feet pointed straight ahead. Running with a duck-like gait can cause shin splints.

■ Proper running surface: Cement is the worst surface, as it is nonresiliant and forces your legs to absorb most of the shock. Asphalt is softer, and grass or dirt is best.

Special risks for women:

Women are generally more flexible, and thus suffer fewer muscular injuries than men. But women must be aware of other hazards of running specific to their sex:

■ The female's wide pelvis and inward-angling thighbones can lead to a chronic case of "runner's knee," a painful condition in which the kneecap rubs against surrounding cartilege. Forty percent of all women runners have knee problems serious enough to require a doctor within the first three months of regular running.

■ An estimated one out of 10 regular female runners stop menstruating (amenorrhea). The condition is generally reversible, and specialists dispute the danger of a lack of cycle. Amenorrhea has been associated with low body fat, although some thin female runners still menstruate. The drop in estrogen production that accompanies amenorrhea has been linked to osteoporosis, or weakening of the bones, a dangerous condition which puts the runner at a greater risk of fracturing her bones.A recent study revealed that women athletes with menstrual problems showed a loss of bone mineral content and bone mass which is normally seen only in older women past menopause. Dr. Barbara Drinkwater of the University of Washington notes that "the bone mass problem concerns only (amenorrheic) women and only those who have been exercising a minimum of a year. The average woman's warning signals are irregular periods."

Dr. Drinkwater also observes that "it appears that younger women are more at risk than older, women who have not had children are more at risk than those who have, those with more intense exercise programs are more at risk than others. And there are women who fit none of these categories who are amenorrheic."

To reduce the risk of osteoporosis, female runners should be sure to consume calcium-rich foods (such as yogurt, cheese and milk) or to take calcium supplements. Calcium supplements vary; calcium carbonate has one of the highest concentrated sources of calcium. Avoid bone meal and dolomite which may contain lead or other toxic metals.

Iron Deficiency

Iron can be lost in urine, feces, heavy perspiration and menstrual blood. As it is difficult to get enough iron through diet, supplements may be necessary. An estimated 55.6 percent of runners have some degree of iron deficiency. Iron is difficult to absorb, and runners may absorb even less because their rapid digestion passes food through the body more quickly than normally. To increase absorption of iron supplements, take them on an empty stomach with vitamin C about a half hour before a meal. Cook food in iron pans—it can increase iron amount up to 5 times. Tea and coffee, and protein in milk, cheese and eggs can decrease iron absorption. Runners may also destroy iron carrying red blood cells in their feet as they repeatedly hit the pavement. Properly cushioned running shoes can help, as can following the golden rule for all sports and gradually increasing level of athletic activity.

Running and the heart

The recent death of running guru Jim Fixx, who died from a heart attack during a daily run, raised some concern over the strain of physical exercise on the heart, but most specialists agree that greater risks of ill-health and premature death await those who **don't** move rather than those who do.

In a Rhode Island Study of men who died while jogging, 42 percent had coronary heart disease. For runners without heart disease, the risk of dying mid-jog is about one in 14,000. It's safe to say that sitting at home is taking a greater risk in terms of heart disease.

Dr. Kenneth Cooper, a cardiologist, recommends a safe but effective program of running three miles in less than 24 minutes five times a week for maximum aerobic benefit and minimum body stress.

Other Running Hazards

A survey taken by the Journal of the American Medical Association found that small percentages of runners were hit by thrown objects (such as cans, bottles, ice, liquids, and a rock-filled bag), bitten by dogs, or run into by bicycles or motor vehicles while running.

The Insurance Institute of Highway Safety found that of 60 motor vehicle accidents involving joggers in 1978, 30 joggers were killed. Half of the collisions occurred after dark, and fault was assigned to the jogger as often as to the driver. To avoid this risk, wear reflective clothing at night, and use your judgement about running with or against traffic—runners have been hit in both cases. Try to stay out of the road altogether.

Pollution

A study in New York measured carboxyhemoglobin (which indicates carbonmonoxide exposure) in the blood of runners before and after a half hour run along a New York expressway at rush hour and found that their levels of COHb tripled. The level in people standing alongside the road also tripled, but reached lower peaks. *Running for half hour in an urban area can produce exposure to carbon monoxide equivalent to smoking one-half to one pack of cigarettes a day.* Although runners in the experiment had to breathe more polluted air than most people would tolerate, you can only benefit by limiting your running to more bucolic settings.

Swimming

Swimming is an ideal exercise for many people. Unlike jogging or tennis, swimming is not a weight-bearing exercise, and therefore ideal for injured athletes and the elderly. Swimming works all the major muscle groups in the body, helps loosen stiff, arthritic, joints and can help prevent varicose veins by improving muscle tone.

The risks of swimming

Swimmer's itch: tender red splotches on the skin. "Aesteatotic eczema" is not an allergic reaction to chlorine, but overdry skin. Chlorine cannot penetrate the skin, but it does dry out the skin's natural oils. If not treated, the problem only worsens because chlorine irritates already dry skin. Dermatologists recommend washing with a mild soap after swimming, and then moisturizing damp skin with lotion. Special "swimmers' creams" are unnecessary.

Swimmer's eye: Chemicals in pool water may also sting the eyes. Swimming in pond water may give you conjunctivitis, or pinkeye, which requires treatment with an antibiotic ointment. Protect your eyes by wearing goggles, and avoid sharing towels to prevent spreading infection.

Swimmer's ear: In swimmer's ear, the skin of outer ear becomes infected, causing pain, itch, and a humming sound. Frequent swimmers should wipe their ears with either a vinegar, alcohol or boric acid solution (use a cotton ball, not a Q-Tip), or put drops of the solution in the ears after swimming. Ear plugs may also prevent ear problems. NOTE: infections of the inner ear are more serious and require medical attention. If a gentle pull to your ear lobe increases the pain, the outer ear is affected. If you feel no increase in pain, the inner ear may be infected and you should see a doctor.

Swimmer's knee: Twenty five percent of competitive swimmers suffer from knee pain. Unless you whip your legs hard while doing the breaststroke, the average recreational swimmer has little risk of developing knee problems from swimming.

Safety: Each year, 6,000 to 8,000 people drown in the U.S., and another million *almost* drown. To avoid tragedy, never swim alone or plunge directly into very cold water; avoid alcohol or eating a meal before swimming; never dive into shallow water, and stay out of the water during a thunderstorm.

Racquet Sports

About 75 million Americans play some kind of racquet sport. The racquet sports, especially the more vigorous games such as squash and racquetball, work the legs and lungs, and require hand-eye coordination and quick reflexes. People who find jogging or swimming laps a bore may enjoy the more sociable aspect of racquet sports.

Eye injuries

Anyone who's played a rousing game of racquetball or squash knows the potential for eye injury. These games are played at fast pace in an enclosed court and it is not uncommon for players to get smacked by the ball or an opponent's racket. Many high-quality, shatterproof eye protectors are available which, if worn, could make the difference between sight or blindness. Don't gamble with this precious sense.

Tennis Elbow: Tennis elbow plagues about half of all tennis players aged 30 and over at some time. Knitters and violinists can get tennis elbow too, which emphasizes that the problem can often originate in the wrist. Tennis elbow is an inflammation of tendons in the outer forearm, and the pain can stretch from the elbow to the fingers. Beginners often suffer tennis elbow because of improper backhand stroke.

Prevention of Tennis Elbow:
- Hit forehand with bent arm.
- Do not hold racquet too tightly.
- Start serving at the shoulder, which is a rotating joint, rather than at the elbow, which is a hinge joint. Tennis elbow usually occurs when you ask your elbow to act as a rotating joint.
- Do not place thumb behind the grip on backhands. Keep it wrapped around handle.
- Don't lead backhand with your elbow and with trunk leaned away from net. Move body weight forward and use shoulder muscle.
- Don't try to put a topspin on the ball by rolling the racquet over the ball, which puts excessive strain on the wrist and asks the elbow to function as a rotating joint.
- Don't swing too hard. Practice to perfect your timing. Hitting the ball too late stresses the forearm.
- Don't toss the ball too high on serves.
- If you're playing on cement, the ball could hit your racquet with too great a force.
- Make sure your racquet is right for you, that it is not too heavy, that the grip is the right size, and that it is not strung too tightly.

Court Surfaces:
Clay courts, cushioned courts and grass courts are kindest to legs and feet. Hard courts are more jarring to the legs and require supportive shoes.

Skiing

The classic ski injury—the broken leg—is rarely seen around the slopes these days; one resort reported only one injury per 100,000 skiers at one resort. The injury rate of skiers has dropped sharply in the past 20 years, from 7.6 injuries per 1,000 skiers in 1960 to 2.2 per 1,000 in 1980, thanks to supportive boots and better release systems in ski bindings. Ankle and shin injuries have declined 60 to 90 percent since 1972. Of the 12 million skiers in the U.S., about three percent have a ski-related accident per year. Knees are still vulnerable to sprains, strains and fractures, but thumbs top the list, as they are frequently injured in falls or caught in a ski handle. Beginners, not surprisingly, suffer more injuries than experienced skiers. At one resort, new skiers suffered 55 percent of the injuries while they only represented 21 percent of the skiers.

Skiing fatalities

Each year in the U.S. about 30 people die in skiing accidents. Ironically, the improved ski equipment which has led to fewer injuries overall also encourages skiers to go faster. The faster the speed, the greater the chance of more serious injury and death.

The majority of skiers killed in 1984 were young, male, and skiing too fast, according to the National Ski Areas Association. The frequency of accidents picks up in the afternoon, when skiers become more confident, but also more tired and less proficient at stopping or turning to avoid obstacles. More than half of the deaths in 1984 were caused by hitting trees.

Preventing ski injuries:

The Consumer Product Safety Commission recommends the following guidelines to assure safe skiing:

■ Any beginner should get expert instruction. Many experts recommend a minimum of five lessons to familiarize the new skier with the basic turns and give him the right amount of confidence—neither too much or too little.

■ Properly fitted equipment is a must. The beginner should rely on a reputable ski shop for the fitting and adjusting of ski equipment.

■ Beginning skiers should use a soft, low boot rather than the high stiff boot often preferred by experts, which can cause severe leg injuries in a fall.

■ Boots must be properly fitted. Don't buy boots too large for children in an attempt to economize. You may end up paying more in medical bills.

■ Bindings must release easily enough to free the skier from serious injury, but not so easily as to cause an unnecessary fall. All bindings should have at least two releasing components—one for a forward fall and one when great twisting forces are applied to the skier's leg.

■ Have your boots with you when you buy bindings to assure compatibility. Make sure you can twist the toe of your boot out of the binding and lift the heel free of the binding using only the leg muscles.

■ Skis should be marked for each foot and should not be interchanged, since a binding that matches the right boot may not match the left boot.

■ Clean bindings and anti-friction devices thoroughly at the beginning of each day's skiing.

■ Don't ski beyond your ability.

■ Don't stop in the middle of a slope. Look both ways before crossing a trail.

■ After a fall, fill in any depressions in the snow made by your body or equipment. Holes or bumps are very hazardous to skiers who follow down the slope.

Cross country skiing

Three million people go cross-country skiing in the U.S. Cross country, or Nordic, skiing is generally much safer than alpine, or downhill, skiing. The U.S. Nordic team records very few injuries, while about 84 percent of alpine ski racers suffer at least one serious injury during their careers. Cold is the biggest problem for cross country skiers, who often sweat considerably and can lose heat through wet clothes if they do not dress properly. (See the **Risks of Winter Sports** in this chapter.)

Although cross country skiers suffer about half as many traumatic injuries as alpine skiers, the sport still poses risks of joint damage, such as ankle sprains and the previously mentioned "skier's thumb." Female skiers seem prone to injuries of the knee ligaments, which they can guard against by strengthening the quadricep muscles (in the front of thigh) with weight training exercises, such as doing leg raises while wearing ankle weights.

Bicycling

Nearly a quarter of all Americans ride bikes. Bicycling is a particularly safe sport, and may even offer more aerobic benefit than running or cross country skiing. Doctors often recommend that injured runners take up cycling to maintain their fitness level while sparing their legs the relentless pounding on the pavement.

About 1,000 U.S. cyclists die in bike accidents per year, three-fourths of them from brain injuries. Most of these victims are children under 16 years old, and in over half the cases, the cyclist was at fault. That means that many accidents could be prevented by teaching children proper rules of safety. Cyclists must legally obey the same rules of the road that cars do.

Only 12 percent of the cycling accidents involve motor vehicles. Most accidents are caused by falling or colliding with dogs or other cyclists.

Precautions:

- Wear a hard-shell helmet.
- Ride on the right side of the road and as close to the right curb as possible, and forget the perceived advantage of being able to see oncoming traffic. It's against the law and confusing to drivers, which makes it dangerous for you.
- Install reflectors and powerful headlights on your bike, and wear reflective clothing during darker hours.
- Watch out for *parked* as well as moving cars. A suddenly opened door may send you flying.
- Wear glasses or sports eye guards to protect your eyes from kicked up dirt and gravel.
- Dogs are a common headache for bikers. Some dogs will actually run right in front of your wheels. Talking firmly may help if you can't outrun a dog which is chasing you. Stopping and slowly walking your bike may also quiet them.
- Ride on bike paths where possible.

 **Play ball!**

The U.S. Consumer Product Safety Commission estimates that over 230,000 people receive emergency room treatment for injuries associated with football every year. Most injuries occur in high school and college sports activities, and half of the injuries occur during practice. The Safety Commission considers football, in terms of frequency and severity of injury, more hazardous than any other sport.

At the same time, football safety has increased significantly over the years. High school football deaths, for example, have dropped from about 2 per 100,000 players in the mid-sixties, to about 0.4 per 100,000 today. Newly adopted rules prohibiting "spearing" an opponent with a helmet helped to lower the incidences of crippling from 32 in 1976 to 11 in 1977.

Strains/sprains and contusions/abrasions together account for about 60 percent of football injuries. Fractures account for about 21 percent of injuries. A little more than 2 percent of injured players require hospitalization.

107

According to the "Forty-third Annual Survey of Football Fatalities," about 10 players die each year from heart failure or heat stroke, while about 19 players die from head and neck injuries. The majority of the fatal accidents occurred in high school games, followed by sandlot games and then college games.

Baseball injuries number over 400,000 per year, although most are not very serious. Baseball is, however, one of the major causes of eye injuries in children.

Soccer

A study by Dr. Frank Noyes of the Cincinnati Sports Medicine and Orthopedic Center uncovered some interesting facts about soccer injuries:

- Soccer players have one-fifth to one-half the injury rate of football players.
- Knees and ankles are injured in one-third of the cases.
- Minor injuries such as bruises often precede major injuries to ankles and knees.
- The player who fouls by knocking down another player is actually injured more frequently than the knocked down player.
- Many soccer players have weak inner thigh muscles which make them more prone to injury.

Female soccer players suffer twice as many game-related injuries as males. Dr. Noyes believes that females may suffer more injuries because they are not as well-trained as the males, and that their injuries are more serious because they tend to be "looser-jointed" than males.

Weight lifting

Weight lifting injuries requiring emergency room visits top 35,000 per year, according to the Consumer Product Safety Commission. Half of those injured are from 10 to 19 years old, and most of the injuries occur at home. The lower back, shoulder and knees are common sites of injury.

Young weight lifters take a particular risk when they workout with very heavy weights, the strain of which can interfere with normal bone development. The bones in the spine and limbs are not fully developed before ages 25 to 30. Weight lifters may also experience a blackout while straining and drop the weight, causing injury. Parents are advised to be cautious about overzealous or overly competitive youngsters who attempt to lift beyond their ability.

Aerobic dance

Half of all aerobic dancers are injured, usually because of overexercising, improper footwear, or working out on hard floors. The most common injuries reported in a recent study of 1,123 female and 164 male aerobic students and instructors were shin splints (28 percent), foot injuries (12 percent) and lower back problems (9.5 percent). Only 100 of the injuries required a physician. The study also found:

■ Those who exercise over 3 times a week increase the risk of injury.

■ Barefoot dancers were injured 65 percent of the time, those wearing running shoes 54 percent of the time, and those with court shoes (tennis or racquetball) 41 percent of the time.

■ 50 percent of those dancing on carpet laid over concrete were injured; 38 percent on hardwood floors, and 36 percent on a heavily padded carpet.

Greater thrill, greater risk?

Fans of more perilous sports such as parachuting and hang gliding probably know the risks of their sport better than most amateur athletes. Knowing the risks may make the activity that more exhilerating. The toll can be high: according to the National Safety Council, about one in 400,000 die playing football each year, while one in 2,308 are killed hang gliding. Parachuters have even higher death rates, with one in 1,207 dying each year. Scuba diving kills about one in 22,000 divers a year. Boxers have a higher death rate than water skiers, with one in 42,000 killed by injuries in the rink compared to one in 380,000 killed in water skiing accidents.

Chapter Eleven
Victims of Crime: Who's at risk?

Most of us share the fear of becoming a victim of crime, and legitimately so—*one in three* American households are subjected to violent or theft crimes each year. You have a greater risk of becoming the victim of violent crime than of getting divorced or dying from cancer. Your particular risk of course depends on many factors, including who you are, where you are, and what you do to protect yourself.

Who you are

■ Young black males are the most frequent victims of crime. One out of five black males aged 16 to 19 becomes the victim of a violent or theft crime each year.[1]

■ Elderly white females are least likely to be victims of violent crime, with one in 42 women aged 65 and older victimized in a year. Although the media often reports crime against women and the elderly, males and the young are actually victimized more often. Women and the elderly may be more sensitized to the possibility of crime and restrict their activities to avoid exposure to dangerous situations.

■ Violent crime rates are higher for divorced and single people, for lower income households, for students and for the unemployed, than for married people, housewives, retirees, or the employed.

■ Hispanics are more often the victims of household crimes than non-Hispanics.

■ Renters are more often victims of household crime than home owners, perhaps because home owners pay more attention to preventive measures such as adequate locks and proper maintenance.

■ Violent crime by strangers affects men, blacks and young people the most, while women face a greater risk than men of becoming the victim of assaults by acquaintances and relatives.

■ When the assailant is a relative, the victim is more likely to suffer serious injuries than when the assailant is an acquaintance or stranger. This finding may be influenced by the possibility that victims of family violence may only report the most serious of these incidents.

Where you are

■ Crime rates are highest in the West, lowest in Central and Appalachian regions of the U.S. Nevada had the highest crime rate in 1982, followed by Florida, California, and Colorado. West Virginia had the lowest crime rate, followed by North Dakota, South Dakota, and Pennsylvania.

■ In 1983, crime touched 32.5 percent of urban households, 28.4 percent of suburban, and 21.6 percent of rural households, according to a Justice Department report. Very urban or resort areas have the highest crime rates; very rural areas have the lowest. Cities plagued by the most crime include New York City; Baltimore, Maryland; Washington, D.C.; and Detroit, Michigan. Cities with lower crime rates include Philadelphia, Pennsylvania; Indianapolis, Indiana; Chicago, Illinois; and San Diego, California. The lowest crime rate of these cities, however, is still one crime per 18 people annually in Philadelphia as opposed to one crime per 8 people in Detroit. Resort areas with high crime rates include Atlantic County, New Jersey; Nantucket, Massachusetts; and Summit County, Colorado.

What you do to protect yourself

■ Criminals look for vulnerable targets. You want to do everything you can to prevent a criminal from classifying you as an "easy rip-off." Your basic task is to *stay alert.* Too often, especially while travelling in train stations or airports, our minds are on time-tables and we are not sufficiently aware of our immediate surroundings. Dress so that you can move easily. If you must wear high heels, carry a pair of more sensible shoes for walking in the street. Avoid drinking too much—if your intoxication doesn't attract a mugger, it will hinder your ability to respond effectively.

Find out about high-crime areas before you travel to a new place. Always lock your car doors and close your windows if you drive through these areas. If you are on foot, walking in the street facing traffic makes it harder for an assailant to jump you from an alley.

Most important: walk with a solid, confident stride, aware of your surroundings.

111

■ When confronted by a criminal, victims who either use physical force, try to attract attention or do nothing at all to protect themselves or their property are most likely to suffer serious injury. On the other hand, victims who try to talk their way out of their predicament (or take non-violent evasive action, such as running away) are least likely to be seriously injured by an assailant, according to the National Crime Survey.

If confronted by an attacker with a weapon, most experts recommend that you stay calm and cooperate with the person. You may be able to negotiate with him. Some women have avoided rape by telling the rapist they were menstruating, or had V.D. or cancer. Pleading is generally *not* a good idea, as it reinforces the power of the assailant and the meekness of the victim.

Will carrying a weapon or other crime-deterrent device help? Controversy still rages over the value of owning a handgun for self-protection. In an assault, if you are not quick enough, your attacker may disarm you and use your weapon against you. You may not be able to reach your Mace or tear gas in time, or again, the attacker may use it against you. Loud whistles or shriek alarms may work by startling your attacker and giving you the extra moment needed to escape. Skunk bombs, which release a truly foul smell, may also disgust your assailant sufficiently to allow you time to get away. Carrying an umbrella or walking stick may discourage an attacker from approaching you in the first place.

Obviously, there is no formula that works in every situation. You cut your risk of injury and theft the most by preventing crime. The following sections look at ways to avoid victimization through prevention.

Car Theft

Over one million Americans found an empty parking space or driveway where they expected to find their cars in 1983. 10 cars are stolen every five minutes, resulting in about one home in fifty losing a car to theft each year. As with most criminals, the car thief tries to make his job as easy as possible, and often it is as easy as opening the door and turning the key: one out of five stolen cars have the keys in them.

The typical car thief of the late 50's was the teenage joyrider, and the recovery rate of stolen cars was as high as 90 percent. Now, according to the National Automobile Theft Bureau, motor vehicle theft has become more of a professional operation, and the nation's third most profitable crime (after drug trafficking and arson). Today, only about half of all stolen cars are recovered.

What car you drive

High Risk of Theft		Low Risk	
BMW 320i	845	Ford Escort Wagon	21
Chevrolet Corvette	791	Pontiac 2000	22
Ford Thunderbird	701	Mercury Lynx	22
Audi 5000	625	Ford Escort 4-door	24
VW Scirocco	610	Ford Escort 2-door	27
Ford Mustang	171	Chevrolet Cavalier	28
Chevrolet Monte Carlo	140	Plymouth Horizon	29
Buick Regal	128	Chevrolet Chevette	33
Chevrolet Camaro	128	Buick Century	46
Oldsmobile Cutlass	123		

Source: Highway Loss Data Institute   **1982 Cars**

For the above cars, 100 represents the average rate of theft for all 1982 models. With an index of 845, for example, BMW's are stolen at a rate 8.45 times higher than average, while the Ford Escort wagons are stolen only one-fifth as often as average. Vans, standard sized pickup trucks, and small and intermediate sized trucks are stolen more often than passenger cars. Car thieves prey most often on sports and specialty models, and least often on station wagons.

Where you leave it

Stolen car rates are highest in Massachusetts, Rhode Island, Michigan and California, and lowest in North and South Dakota, Mississippi, and Iowa.

Most cars are stolen after dark, particularly between 8 and 10 p.m. Thieves often stalk shopping center parking lots as well as neighborhood streets; often the stolen car was parked in the owner's driveway or nearby.

To avoid motor vehicle theft

■ The simple advice which would prevent almost 20 percent of auto thefts if heeded: lock your car and pocket your key.

■ Professional thieves may drive up to your car in a tow truck in broad daylight and calmly hook it up in front of passersby. Turn your front wheels sharply to the left or right to make towing more difficult. Lock your wheels when you park by setting the emergency brake and leaving the transmission in "Park" for automatic transmissions; for a stick shift, set the emergency brake and leave the transmission in gear.

■ Conceal valuables you leave in your car, as well as anything that might appear valuable. A suitcase, though you know contains only dirty clothes and the sweater your sweetheart knitted, may encourage a thief to break into your car. If you have a tape deck, insure it, and get a special lock or a fake AM-radio face plate to conceal it.

■ Don't leave the car's title and other documents that identify it in the glove compartment. Most states require you to show your registration if stopped by a policeman, so you should keep it in your wallet rather than the glove box.

■ Give only your ignition key to parking lot attendants. If you leave your housekeys, the attendant has an opportunity to duplicate them and use them himself or sell them to a professional burglar.

■ Good auto theft alarms cost between $150 to $400. This option may be for you if you feel your car has a high risk of being stolen. Some systems include pagers to alert the owner when the car alarm goes off.

■ "Comprehensive" auto insurance insures against vehicle theft. Property insurance is necessary to cover any valuables stolen with the car.

Burglary

Six million households (7 percent of homes in U.S.) were burglarized at least once in 1981. In nearly three million of these burglaries, the burglar gained entry by going through an unlocked door or window, or by using a key from under a doormat. Of these "no-force" entries, 34 percent took place during the day. According to a Justice Department study, the typical burglar lives within a mile of the home he burglarizes.

In a recent year in the U.S., most burglaries occurred in the West, with Nevada claiming the most (between 2 and 3 burglaries per 100 households), followed by Florida and California. North and South Dakota suffered the fewest burglaries, with less than one-half of a percent of the households victimized. In 1983, 8.5 percent of black households were burglarized, and 5.8 percent of white households.

Burglary is a crime of opportunity. You do not need to own expensive jewelry or furs to attract burglars. In fact, people with low incomes (less than $3,000 per year) are victimized as often as high income people (more than $25,000 per year). The most common items stolen are radios, sports equipment, tape recorders, stereos, clothes—anything which can be removed easily and sold easily. Burglars look for homes vulnerable to the quickest, quietest break-in possible. You want your home to appear occupied and well secured to discourage burglars from choosing your home in the first place, as well as installing the necessary hardware to make your home difficult to break into.

Come rob my home

Reduce the risk that a burglar will even consider your home as a target for burglary:

■ Keep doors and windows as visible as possible. High fences or bushes just give intruders a place to hide and work undisturbed. Try planting low bushes which have thorns or spines, like rose bushes.

■ If you must leave your keys with your car in a garage or lot, always separate the car and house keys. Don't leave identification on your key ring.

■ Install lights outside your home.

■ Don't leave notes on outside doors such as "Gone to store, back at 3 p.m." which let intruders know your home is unoccupied.

■ Don't let unknown callers know you are alone.

■ Don't give a burglar the tools for his trade by leaving out ladders or other tools.

■ Avoid using your address in classified advertising. Burglars also read the newspaper—ads, social event announcements and obituaries can tell a burglar where and when homes will be empty.

■ Participate in your local Operation Identification. Your local police department will lend you an electric engraver to mark your valuables, and then give you a sticker to display which lets burglars know you are security conscious. Items marked with your social security number will be easier to identify as stolen goods.

■ Be cautious in conversation with those who have no need to know about your financial situation.

That "lived-in" look

■ A small mailbox overflowing with mail lets a burglar know your out. Get a larger mailbox or install a mail slot in your door.

■ Keep your garage door closed and cover garage windows.

■ If you're going to be out for a short while, turn on the lawn sprinkler or use a water timer.

Vacation tips

■ When you go away on trips, ask a neighbor to watch your house, pick up your mail, and if the family has a second car, to park it in your driveway. You want your home to appear "lived in," so stop your newspaper delivery, leave the shades in different positions, put your lights on timers.

■ Ask a friend or neighbor to mow your lawn, shovel the snow or rake the leaves.

■ Hide your garbage cans in your basement or storage shed. Empty cans when others in the neighborhood have full cans is a tip to the burglar that no one's home.

■ Turn the bell on your telephone down low, so a burglar around your house won't hear the rings go unanswered.

Securing your home

■ If someone lived in your house or apartment before you, have the cylinders in the locks changed.

■ Remember that the strongest lock cannot protect a flimsy door. Outside doors should be solid core or metal. If you live in a high-risk area, reinforce the door jamb with steel strips.

■ Replace key-in-knob locks, which are easily broken, with high quality rim locks, or supplement existing locks with a jimmy-proof vertical dead bolt (see figure 1).

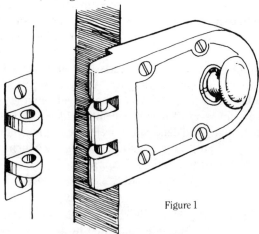

Figure 1

If your home has any panes of glass within 40 inches of a door knob, either cover the glass with grillwork, replace it with plexiglass, or use a quality deadbolt lock with a double cylinder deadbolt which requires keys inside and out (see figure 2).

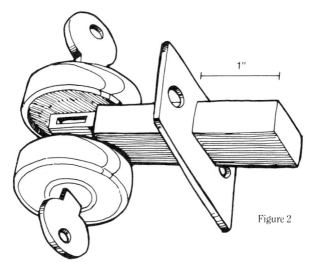

Figure 2

■ Secure sliding glass patio doors by installing protruding screw heads in grooves over the door to prevent lifting the door out (leave enough room to let the door slide). Or drill a hole and insert a nail through the inside frame and part way through the door frame. You can remove the nail from inside. Other methods include laying a broom in the floor track or using a slide bolt with a key (see figures).

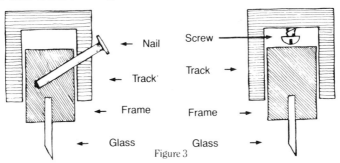

Figure 3

■ Install a peep-hole. They are quite inexpensive and easy to install.

■ Secure double hung windows with key locks, pin methods, or grill work as well as using the latch.

■ Make a list of all merchandise you own with brand name, model and serial number, physical description and estimated value. Take photographs and keep all this information in a safe deposit box.

■ Theft insurance is included in most homeowners' policies, but renters must insure their own personal property. Look for a policy that doesn't require proof of forced entry, and insure property for replacement value rather than cash value. If you cannot afford property insurance, consider Federal Crime Insurance, which is fairly inexpensive. To qualify you must install approved locks on outside doors and windows.

■ Police will inspect your home for free and advise on how to improve security.

Locks

Look at your door locks. If you have a key-in-the-knob type lock, found in 90 percent of new homes, a burglar with the right tool and a few seconds can easily rip the knob off and get to the lock mechanism. The same applies to the mortice locks common in older homes, with the lock mechanism installed in a cavity inside the door, despite their sturdier appearance. Key-in-the-knob locks are so vulnerable it makes sense to replace them entirely with either an interconnected lockset which contains two locks, one in the knob and one mounted above the knob which controls a dead-bolt, both opened by the same key; or vertical bolt locks sold specifically as replacements for primary locks.

If you have the mortice lock, rather than going through the difficulty of removing it, add an auxiliary door lock such as a vertical bolt type or cylinder dead-bolt lock (see figure 1). Make sure the strike plate—the metal plate attached to the door frame which receives the bolt— is attached with 2 1/2" - 3" long screws which will reach the wall studs behind the jamb. Standard strikes which are attached only to the door frame itself can be kicked out easily.

Check your window locks. Most commercially available window locks can be forced easily by hand or pried off with a screwdriver. You can secure your windows yourself more effectively with minimal effort. Just drill through the sashes where they overlap and insert an eyebolt to pin them together (see figure 4). Make sure all members of your family know about the eyebolts and how to remove them in case of fire.

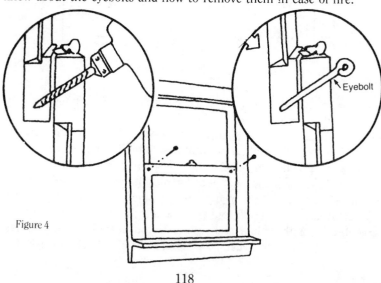

Figure 4

If you confront a burglar...

If, despite your conscientious security measures, a burglar breaks into your home, and you confront him, don't be a hero. Stay calm, and don't try to stop him. A burglar caught in the act is unpredictable. Try to get out yourself and seek help.

If you are coming home and you suspect burglary, don't go in. Call the police from a neighbor's house. Do not touch anything after a burglary until the police have checked your home.

Rape

■ A woman has a one in ten chance of being raped sometime during her life.

■ Every six minutes, a woman is raped somewhere in the U.S.

■ No female, from a two month old infant to a doddering grandmother, is immune to rape. The most common victim is a school-aged girl, and her assailant is generally of the same race and known to her by sight. 40 percent of rapists are friends, acquaintances, or family members.

■ An estimated 165,000 to 700,000 rapes go unreported each year in the United States.

These unpleasant statistics should stress to all women the importance of learning to protect themselves and of educating their daughters to avoid dangerous situations. The list of safety precautions which follows is not meant to reduce women to nervous wrecks the moment they venture outside their home (though the disturbing fact remains that about half of all rapes are committed in the victim's or assailant's home); rather, a woman should walk with purpose and project an image of assertiveness and confidence. Just as a burglar looks for homes easy to break into, a rapist looks for women who appear vulnerable to attack. And just as a homeowner may discourage burglary either before an attempt by making his home appear well-secured, or after an attempt with an effective alarm system, so a woman may prevent rape by avoiding a confrontation all together, or by acting wisely after she has been threatened. Suggestions follow for both cases.

119

How to avoid rape (or any assault)

■ Use only your initials before your last name in the phone book, on a mailbox or public advertisement.

■ When driving alone, keep your doors locked, windows rolled, and convertible top up. If you need fresh air, only open the window next to you.

■ Don't stop for a stranded motorist, even a woman. Notify the police at the nearest opportunity—both of you will probably be better off.

■ Always carry enough change to make a phone call in an emergency.

■ Do not get on an elevator with a suspicious-looking person, or if a suspicious-looking person gets in after you, step out. Stand near the control panel if you are riding with a stranger so you can push the alarm button or get off on a different floor.

■ Learn to prevent situations which could render you helpless: keep your car in good condition to minimize the chance of breaking down and becoming stranded; don't let your gas tank drop below one-quarter full; learn how to change a tire. In other words, learn to be self-sufficient.

■ Don't speak with strangers more than necessary. It's old advice, but unfortunately very valid. Many assailants use the ploys of asking the time or directions, or of dropping an object in a woman's path in order to distract and then corner her.

What should you do if attacked?

Should you scream and struggle, play for time, or submit passively in order to avoid suffering more serious injuries? One problem is that juries will not usually convict a rapist if the woman did not resist. And although resistance and immediate flight can increase your chance of escape, it may also increase your risk of serious injury by angering the rapist as he fears himself losing control. Frederic Storaska, star of the film, *How to Say No to a Rapist and Survive,* advocates thinking your way out, discouraging the use of Mace and weapons as he believes these devices are too easily used against the victim. As a final resort, he recommends squeezing the man's testicles hard to send him into shock. Unfortunately, it is impossible to discern beforehand the proper reaction to an attack. Here are some things to consider:

■ If you believe you might get hurt by defending yourself or if you're afraid to fight back, don't. Submitting to a rape out of fear for your safety or your family's (rapists may threaten to harm the victim's children or other family members), does not mean that you consented. It is still a rape, and still a crime, even if you do not have a single cut or bruise. It should still be reported to the police. Victims who do not resist should never feel guilty: it is the rapist who committed the crime.

■ Passive resistance may help lessen the violence of an attack. Try to calm the attacker. You may be able to discourage him by claiming to be sick or pregnant. Some women have turned off attackers by acting insane, crying hysterically, or forcing themselves to vomit or urinate. Again, this kind of behavior may win you freedom or simply anger the attacker and cause more violent acts. You will have to gauge the situation.

If you're at home, tell the attacker your boyfriend, husband or roomate will be home soon.

■ Some women feel most confident with training in self-defense through martial arts courses such as judo or karate. These techniques can be effective, but proficiency takes a lot of hard practice.

Homicide

Although homicide is the least frequent violent crime, every 23 minutes, one person kills another in the U.S., totalling over 20,000 people a year. The average American's chance of having his life end in homicide is one in 150. In most homicides, the murderer has no criminal record and is acquainted with the person killed. The victim and killer are related in one in six cases, and otherwise acquainted in more than one-third of all homicides. The risk of becoming a murder victim increases when other crimes are involved. One in four homicides occur during commission of another crime, and one in 100 robberies committed with a gun ends in a murder.

Justice Department officials believe there has been an increase in "serial killers," who roam the country searching for victims, and in recreational killers, who, as their name disturbingly implies, kill for "fun," rather than the traditional motives of greed, jealousy or revenge. Serial killers are usually intelligent males who travel a lot, often at night, perhaps covering 150,000 to 200,000 miles a year. They are difficult to catch, as their apparently random murder victims show up in different counties or states with no discernible link.

Handguns

Two-thirds of all homicides are committed with handguns. The gun homicide rate in the U.S. is 50 times higher than that of England, Germany, Denmark and Japan. As a whole, Americans own between 30 and 50 million handguns—more guns per capita than any other country in the world. The gun control issue stirs strong feelings on both sides, but statistics indicate that most homicides are not pre-meditated, and that most killers use the most convenient weapon available. Few of the guns people buy for protection are used for that purpose. One estimate finds six times as many deaths from firearm accidents than from killings of burglars or other intruders. With the exception of National Rifle Association devotees, most homicide researchers believe more guns mean more deaths. Of all assault victims, five times as many people die from gunshot wounds than from knife wounds.

The following graph compares the rate of handgun murders in different countries.

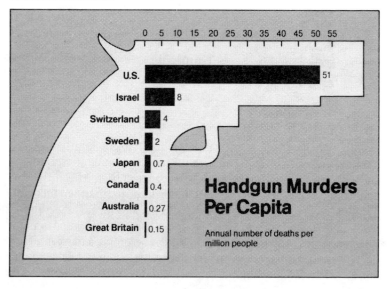

Handgun Murders Per Capita

Annual number of deaths per million people

U.S.	51
Israel	8
Switzerland	4
Sweden	2
Japan	0.7
Canada	0.4
Australia	0.27
Great Britain	0.15

Where you live

In the United States, Alaska has the highest murder rate, with one in 5,400 slain a year. In North Dakota, only one in every 143,000 people are killed annually. Rates are higher in cities: each year one in 2,300 are murdered in Detroit, one in 3,300 in Washington D.C.

The murder rate in the United States, 10 murders per 100,000 citizens, is higher than the rates in 80 percent of the countries that report homicide statistics to the United Nations. South Africa, Nicaragua, and Mexico have higher rates. With 17 murders per 100,000 people, Mexico has one of the highest rates, while Canada has a low 2 murders per 100,000 citizens. France, Great Britain, Switzerland, Sweden, Germany, Denmark, Austria and Norway all have even lower homicide rates than Canada.

Who you are

- Black men are seven times more likely to be murdered than white men, and 22 times more likely than white women. Black women are murdered four times as often as white women.
- Young black men are the most frequent victims of homicide. If a black man dies between the ages of 20 and 24, the chance that he was murdered is higher than one in three.

Arson

Professionally set insurance fraud fires actually account for only a small percentage of arson fires. Most vandalism fires are set by teenagers for "kicks." In fact, two out of every five arson fires are set by children, and the number may be growing. A violent quarrel, a bitter argument between lovers, or the firing of an employee who wants to get back at his company, may motivate an arson for revenge.

Cities with declining populations are the most likely to have high arson rates, as there are more abandoned buildings to attract vandals. Some facts on getting burned: (Source: U.S. Department of Justice)

- Arson is the fastest growing crime: reported arson fires increased more than four-fold between 1965 and 1975.
- Arson fires killed over 1,000 people in 1978.
- Over $1 billion in property loss was a result of arson in 1978.
- About 212,000 arson cases occurred in 1978, with an average $6,533 lost in each fire—higher than for any other major crime.
- A typical city of 100,000 might expect to have about 100 arson fires a year.

To protect your property against arson:
- Clean up anything that could be set afire—old rags, boards, newspapers, etc.

- Store gasoline and other flammable liquids under lock and key.
- Keep your property well-lighted.
- Install smoke alarms. Your fire department may provide advice about alarm systems.

Domestic Violence

To most people, a "criminal" implies a stranger, but actually many victims of assault, rape and murder are attacked by friends or family members. Family members killing each other count for one in five of all homicides in America. Family violence cuts across all social classes. Between one-fifth and one-half of American couples suffer violence *regularly* in their marriages, and three-fifths of all couples will experience violence at least once during their marriages. More police are killed in the line of duty answering family complaints than in any other case, according to the F.B.I.

Woman Battering

Husbands and boyfriends kill nearly a third of all slain women. Attacks by husbands on wives result in more injuries requiring medical treatment than rapes, muggings and automobile accidents *combined.* In fact, women have a three and a half times greater risk of being beaten by their husband than of being assaulted in the street.

Men who beat their wives are often outwardly "good citizens." Often the man will have drunk alcohol before assaulting his wife, although only a small percentage are actually alcoholics. In most cases, the man is dominant in the relationship, has low self-esteem and feels himself under considerable stress. He seems to have a "split personality"—violent and abusive at one time, kind and loving at another. The woman is usually passive and feels helpless to the situation.

The National Institute of Mental Health advises the battered woman to first admit to herself that she is being abused and that she is not being treated fairly. Most communities have hotlines women can call for support and more information about where to get help. Perhaps equally important as individual action by abused wives is community action. That means neighbors reporting any domestic violence they may observe in the next apartment or the house down the street, instead of considering it "none of their business." The observation of the NIMH publication *Wife Abuse* rings true: until society rejects its tolerance and acceptance of violence for resolving conflict and expressing anger, meaningful changes in family relationships will not occur.

Child Abuse

The National Committee for the Prevention of Child Abuse estimates that one million children are abused each year, and that five thousand children die from such abuse. That means that every day almost fourteen children die from abuse-related injury.

About half of all abusive parents were abused themselves as children. Younger parents are more likely to abuse their children than older parents, often because they feel overwhelmed by the responsibilities of parenthood. Unwanted pregnancies leading to premature marriages, financial worries and relationship difficulties are some typical problems which create stress and make child abuse more likely.

The sexually abused child is more prevalent than the physically abused, or battered, child. In one recent study, Diana E. H. Russell, professor of sociology at Mills College, found that about two out of seven girls will be sexually abused before age 14, and nearly two in five will have at least one such experience before age 18.

Accounts of sexual abuse of children have multiplied to a disturbing degree in the past few years. Statistics are difficult to obtain, as many cases go unreported. Some researchers estimate that only about two percent of sexual molestations against pre-school children are ever reported. Estimates of the number of abused children runs from 45,000 to one million. Sen. Christopher Dodd, the founder of the Children's Caucus, states that a child is sexually abused every two minutes in the U.S.

Teachers, babysitters, camp counselors, relatives and family friends may be the abusers, but an estimated 75 percent of all cases involve incest between parents and children. Children who witness abuse or are themselves abused are 1,000 times more likely to abuse someone when they are adults than children who are not abused.

Families in which incest has occurred have been helped by a self help organization called Parents United, which has 90 chapters across the U.S. Write to:

Parents United
P.O. Box 952
San Jose, CA 95108

The best way to reduce the risk of your child being molested is to establish an open and communicative relationship with your child. Teach your child that he or she has the right to refuse any physical contact that is uncomfortable or confusing, and to always let you know if someone approaches or touches him or her in a way that seems wrong, even if the person says to keep it a secret.

125

Chapter Twelve
The Big Killers:
Common Diseases and How to Avoid Them

When we are healthy, we do not like to think about disease. But the way we live often influences the way we die. If we think of illness as something that strikes from outside, apart from us, and medication as something that heals from outside, then we live in a very haphazard world. But when we see illness as a result of certain conditions in our lives, we become able to exercise personal responsibility over our health.

Heart Disease

Over a million Americans suffer heart attacks each year. Heart attacks are the most common sign of coronary heart disease, a disease epidemic among middle-aged and elderly Americans today. In fact, in most industrialized countries, more adults contract coronary heart disease than any other life threatening disease. Nearly one million people died of heart disease in the U.S. in 1984. One in four of those deaths is of a person under age 65.

The grim statistics persist: an American male has a one in five chance of having a heart attack before the age of 65. Of those affected, 25 percent will die instantly or within three hours. 15 percent will die within the first few weeks after the attack. The lucky ones who recover still have five times the risk of dying within the next five years compared with men without coronary heart disease.

Particularly tragic is the well-established fact that many deaths from heart disease could have been prevented by simple changes in personal habits. Quitting smoking, getting blood pressure checked regularly and treated, and reducing intake of high-fat, high-cholesterol foods are all

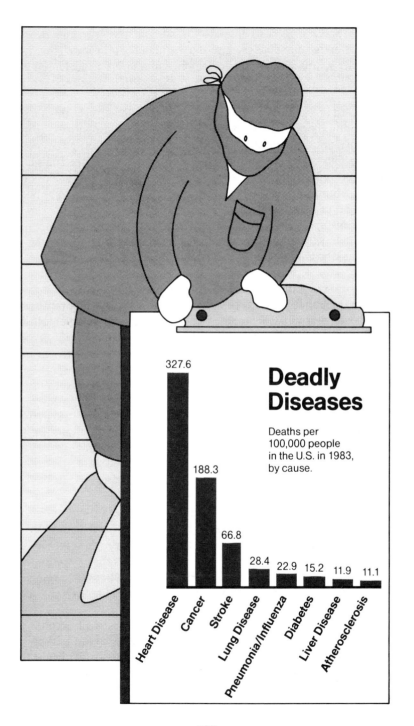

Deadly Diseases

Deaths per 100,000 people in the U.S. in 1983, by cause.

- Heart Disease — 327.6
- Cancer — 188.3
- Stroke — 66.8
- Lung Disease — 28.4
- Pneumonia/Influenza — 22.9
- Diabetes — 15.2
- Liver Disease — 11.9
- Atherosclerosis — 11.1

vital in preventing heart disease. In addition, the American Heart Association recommends exercise and maintaining proper weight. Unfortunately, this well-known, common sense advice is all too often ignored.

Cigarettes: A heartfelt habit?

The list of the dangers of cigarette smoking is long and frightening, longer and more frightening and even more well-substantiated than those of many other substances banned by the Food and Drug Administration. Old habits die hard, especially old habits supported and sustained by multi-million dollar industries with little intention of closing up shop. Smokers continue to smoke, and smokers continue to be two to three times more likely to die from heart attacks than non-smokers. The Surgeon General recently reported that smoking causes more deaths annually from coronary heart disease than from all cancers. Smokers who quit, especially those under 65, can cut their risk up to 45 percent.

Nicotine or carbon monoxide in cigarette smoke can poison the heart muscle and weaken it, leading to a disease called cardiomyopathy, which kills nearly 10,000 people a year, according to a report published in the New England Journal of Medicine. In men under 55, cardiomyopathy is three times as common among heavy smokers as in nonsmokers.

Women smokers have vastly increased their numbers since the 1930s, providing a living demonstration of smoking's nasty effects. According to the Harvard Medical School Health Letter, cigarette smoking may be responsible for two-thirds of the first-time heart attacks suffered by women under age 50.

What You Eat and How Much You Move: Diet and Exercise

An international study of heart disease revealed a correlation between high intake of saturated fat and high rates of heart disease. Men from Eastern Finland and the United States have the highest incidence rates, while Japan, Corfu, Crete and Dalmatia, with their lower-in-fat diets, have much lower rates.(For diet recommendations to maximize your health and lower your chances of contracting many diseases—see Chapter 1)

Regular exercise can cut your risk of heart disease in half, according to a study by Harvard University. Walking two miles a day at a *brisk* pace is sufficient if you don't feel up to more vigorous activity. Studies have found that athletes have lower levels of the "bad" cholesterol—low density lipoproteins (LDL)—and higher levels of the "good" cholesterol—high density lipoproteins (HDL). LDL is cholesterol that clings to artery walls, creating blockage which can lead to heart attacks. HDL helps the body remove cholesterol.

Ideally, exercise coupled with a sound, low-fat diet is the best way to avoid heart disease. But exercise can even better the odds for overweight individuals or average weight people who aren't quite ready to give up their french fries.

Where the Pounds Are

Recent research has found that *where* your extra weight is located affects your chances of getting heart disease. If most of your extra weight is around your waistline, your risk of heart attack could be up to eight times higher than average. A man's health begins to be at risk when his waist measurement equals his hip measurement. Women should take heed once their waistline reaches more than 80 percent of their hip measurement.

A Difference in Attitude

The driven, success-oriented individual who often becomes impatient and aggressive (a "Type A" personality; see Chapter One), has five or more times the risk of developing heart disease than calmer people who are less competitive and more trustful of others. You may have no family history of heart disease, watch your diet and exercise regularly, but if your attitude is too often hostile or hurried, your heart may truly take a beating. A study at the Mt. Zion Hospital found that Type A heart attack victims can cut their risk of getting another heart attack in half when they modify their overly aggressive behavior.

Home is Where the Heart Is

A survey of the United States finds the lowest heart disease death rates in the Mountain and Pacific states, particularly in Alaska, Hawaii, New Mexico, Colorado, Utah, Idaho, Washington, and North Dakota. The death rate for men is about 403 per 100,000; for women, 155 per 100,000. The highest death rates are in the Middle Atlantic and Southern states, with West Virginia, Kentucky, South Carolina, Louisiana, Pennsylvania, New Jersey, New York and Delaware topping the list. An average of 529 men die per 100,000, and about 211 women per 100,000. Dr. Thomas Thom of the National Heart, Lung and Blood Institute speculates that poorer states which lack adequate emergency medical care may contribute to the higher rates.

A study of communities who lived near airports by the University of California at Los Angeles has found that residents 75 years and older had significantly higher heart attack and stroke death rates than residents of less noisy communities. The regular exposure to loud noise from the planes apparently causes enough tension to lead to high blood pressure in some residents.

Some Good News

Although heart disease is still the nation's biggest killer, the number of heart disease deaths have actually dropped since the early sixties. Advances in medical technology have helped, but many doctors believe that people living healthier lives accounts for a large percentage of the drop. More wholesome diets and less cigarette smoking may be the major reasons heart disease mortality rates have dropped in the U.S., Canada and Australia. The numbers are still up, however, in England and Wales, where the diet is high in fat, and smoking has subsided little.

Cancer

Although heart disease is still the nation's biggest killer, cancer seems to be a greater source of fear, perhaps because of its mysteriousness, and its association with a painful wasting away of the body. Anything about cancer is generally newsworthy; anti-cancer diets abound; and the frustrated sentiment that "everything causes cancer" is well known. A child born in the United States today has a one in three chance of developing cancer sometime in life, with a one in four or five chance of dying from it. Two out of three families are touched by cancer.

We may feel immersed in a world of carcinogens, any one of which could deal the fatal blow. Enough is known about cancer, however, that you can significantly reduce your risk of dying from this disease—a study by scientists at Oxford University estimated that 35 percent of cancer in the U.S. was associated with dietary factors, 30 percent with tobacco use, seven percent with reproductive and sexual behavior, three percent with alcohol, three percent with "geophysical factors" such as sunlight, and about ten percent from infection. Cancer is a very complex disease, and susceptibility to cancer-causing agents varies among individuals. But even with the variables, enough *is* known that you can improve your odds against dying of this disease.

Who You Are

White males are most likely to develop some kind of cancer, followed by black males, white women, and finally black women. Black males are more likely to suffer from cancer of the mouth, pharynx, esophagus, larynx, lung and prostate—cancers associated with personal habits such as smoking, poor diets, and excessive alcohol consumption, as well as exposure to carcinogens on the job. Both black and white males most commonly contract cancers of the lung, prostate and colon-rectum.

White women are more likely to develop breast cancer than black women, while black women are more likely to develop cancers of the esophagus and cervix than white women. Women have certainly "come a long way" since 15 years ago, when lung cancer killed only half as many women as it does today. Now lung cancer causes more deaths in women than breast cancer. This substantial increase in lung cancer accompanies the increase in smoking among women since the 1930s. The increased number of women in the workforce may also contribute to the higher rate as more women are exposed to occupational carcinogens.

Common Cancers

Skin Cancer   Skin cancer is the most common cancer, also the most easily treated. Sores that do not heal often signal skin cancer, and about 95 percent of all skin cancer cases could be cured if people with these symptoms promptly sought medical care. Exposure to too much sunlight, X-rays, radium, coal, arsenic, creosote, lignite and petroleum by-products can all lead to skin cancer. In the United States, more people suffer from skin cancer in the South than in the North. Farmers and sailors have a higher incidence than many other occupations, and light skinned people are more vulnerable than darker skinned people.

Breast Cancer   Breast cancer strikes about 115,000 women in the United States each year, killing nearly one third of them. Women over 40 make up 80 percent of all breast cancer victims, and women with breast cancer in the family have a higher risk than other women. Other factors which may influence whether a woman develops breast cancer:

■ Women who have borne children appear to have less risk of breast cancer than childless women, possibly due to a hormonal factor.

■ Women who have given birth before age 18 may also have a reduced risk of breast cancer.

■ Women who give birth for the first time after age 35, however, are more at risk than childless women.

■ Overweight women and Jewish women of European descent are considered at a higher risk.

■ Women who took DES during their pregnancies to prevent miscarriages have a 47 percent greater chance of developing breast cancer than non-DES women, according to a recent study at Dartmouth University.

Self-examination of the breasts can significantly reduce a woman's risk of dying from breast cancer. A study at the Vermont Regional Cancer Center found that 90 percent of breast cancer patients who self-examined their breasts had found their own tumors, allowing them to receive treatment a crucial six months earlier than woman who did not examine their own breasts. In addition, the women who found their own tumors had a 20 percent greater chance of surviving the cancer than the other women.

131

Colon Cancer   Colon cancer strikes about 120,000 Americans each year. The disease kills more people than breast cancer: sixty thousand die of it annually. The risk of colon cancer increases with age, with most cases in people 55 to 75 years old.

What affects your risk of developing colon cancer?

■ If you have a family history of polyps in the rectum, be sure to get regular examinations starting in your thirties.

■ Up to one-third of people who have had ulcerative colitis develop colon cancer.

■ People working in sedentary jobs, such as bookkeepers, bus drivers, and computer programmers, are more likely to develop colon cancer than people in more physically active occupations, such as auto mechanics and plumbers. If your job keeps you in your seat most of the day, make time to exercise after work.

■ If you eat a diet high in fat and beef and low in fiber, you may increase your chances of developing colon cancer. Eat more grains and vegetables to get the roughage that keeps your digestive system functioning efficiently.

Lung Cancer   Lung cancer causes more deaths than any other cancer. 139,000 Americans are stricken with lung cancer each year, and about 121,000 die of it. Smokers have a 10 times greater risk of developing lung cancer than nonsmokers. Smokers who quit can dramatically reduce their risk. Ten to fifteen years after quitting, the risk of lung cancer drops to about the level of a nonsmoker's.

Occupational exposure to substances such as asbestos, uranium and dyes can also lead to lung cancer.

Nightcaps, Paint Thinner, Hormones and Other Risks

■ Drinking too much alcohol increases the risk of cancers of the esophagus, mouth, throat, larynx and liver.

■ X-rays should only be given if they are a key part of diagnosis or treatment. People who received X-ray treatments involving the head or neck as children should have their thyroid glands examined by a doctor.

■ Exposure to certain chemicals in industry can pose a cancer risk to workers. Such chemicals include asbestos, aniline dyes, arsenic, chromium, nickel compounds, vinyl chloride, benzene, and certain products of coal, lignite, oil shale and petroleum. People who work with hazardous chemicals should always follow proper safety procedures.

■ Avoid long exposure to household solvent cleaners, cleaning fluids, and paint thinners. Always work in a well-ventilated area when using these products.

■ Daughters of women who took DES, a drug to prevent miscarriages, have a higher risk of developing cancers of the vagina and cervix. Both mothers and daughters should get yearly breast and pelvic exams and Pap tests.

Hypertension

Hypertension, or high blood pressure affects 60 million people in the U.S. Hypertension increases the risk of heart attack, stroke, kidney and eye problems. Although headache, chest pain, shortness of breath and heart palpitations can signal hypertension, you may also feel nothing and still have high blood pressure. Pressure should be checked regularly.

Your risk of high blood pressure is increased if you have a family history of hypertension, you are older, male or black, you are overweight, smoke, or use oral contraceptives. Proper weight, proper diet, and proper exercise are the basic trio for treating hypertension. Excess weight means an excess burden on the heart. Exercise, besides aiding in weight loss, strengthens the heart muscle and increases circulation.

Cutting down on sodium can also help control high blood pressure, although sodium alone is not the demon it's made out to be. High blood pressure depends on a complicated interplay of calcium, sodium, zinc, lead and other minerals. Low calcium consumption could be as dangerous as high sodium intake. A study reported in the Journal of the American College of Cardiology found that calcium supplementation in hypertensive individuals with low calcium levels helped lower their blood pressure.

Another study at the University of Michigan found that people with higher blood pressures tended to have higher than average levels of lead in the blood, though still within the normal range. Leaded-gas products or automobile emissions are two sources of lead exposure. A diet high in potassium is often necessary to counteract hypertensive medications which can deplete the body's potassium supply. Foods high in potassium include bananas, dates, raisins, baked potatoes, lamb and pork chops, peanut butter, walnuts, cottage cheese, and yogurt.

Alcohol and caffeine consumption are not recommended for people with high blood pressure.

Stroke

The American Heart Association estimates that more than 164,000 people die of stroke each year, while another 2 million survive but suffer disabilities ranging from a reduced command of language to the inability to use the bathroom alone. Stroke is the third largest cause of death in the United States, although the AHA recently announced that the stroke death rate has dropped a "dramatic 45 percent" in the past 16 years, thanks to improved detection and better treatment of high blood pressure.

During a stroke brain cells are deprived of blood, causing neurological damage which is usually irreversible. The first stroke is unfortunately rarely the last stroke—more are likely to follow in the future, so the wisest action is to prevent the conditions which can precede stroke—heart disease, high blood pressure, diabetes and high cholesterol level.

Every one of the estimated 37 million people in America with high blood pressure is a stroke candidate; having blood pressure checked regularly is one of the simplest and most important precautions a person can take.

Diet and Stroke

The high-fiber, low-sodium, low-fat diet recommended in Chapter One for all health-conscious individuals has been found to reduce blood pressure and make antihypertensive drugs unnecessary for some people suffering from both high blood pressure and diabetes. (*Postgraduate Medical Journal,* October, 1983) Diabetics have about double the risk of stroke as non-diabetics. Particularly important for stroke prevention is adequate calcium intake, and decrease or elimination of salt and caffeine from the diet. Supplementation with magnesium and vitamin C may also be helpful. Exercise is also important—a study in the Netherlands found that people who exercise regularly have less than half the risk of stroke as their sedentary counterparts.

The risk of stroke for smokers is about five times higher than for nonsmokers. Cerebral blood flow is lower in smokers, and gets lower as more cigarettes are smoked.

Stroke is a *preventable* disease, not an inevitable consequence of aging. Doctors believe that with new, simpler and cheaper tests to identify potential stroke victims, coupled with sound nutrition and proper exercise, 50 to 75 percent of the strokes today could be prevented.

Osteoporosis

One in four women over age 60 suffer from osteoporosis, a crippling, bone-thinning disease. Osteoporosis begins to develop early in life, as the bones silently begin to thin out about age 35, afflicting many more women than men. The bone loss accelerates after menopause, when the amount of estrogen in the body, which appears to inhibit bone loss, decreases.

The thinned bones are then vulnerable to fracture, even from such mild activity as making a bed or opening a window. A fracture is usually the first sign of the disease. A woman over 50 is about seven times more likely to fracture her forearm than a 40-year-old. Osteoporosis causes about 200,000 broken hips a year. Most of the victims are over 70, and up to one-fifth of them will die of complications from the fracture within four months, while up to one-half will be unable to continue living independently.

The most likely candidates for osteoporosis:

■ Fair-skinned white women. Black women generally have denser bones and thus a lower incidence of the disease.

■ Thin women and those with small bone structure.

■ Women with a family history of the disease.

■ Women who have had their ovaries removed at an early age.

■ Women who have an early menopause lose estrogen's protective effect earlier, putting them at a higher risk.

■ Heavy smokers, and drinkers of alcohol or caffeine may be accelerating their rate of bone loss.

■ High protein diets can lead to excessive calcium excretion and a resulting weakening of the bones. A comparison of vegetarian and meat-eating women in one study revealed that meat-eating women lost about twice as much bone as lacto-ovo-vegetarian women (those who do not eat meat, but do eat eggs and milk products).

135

Outward signs of osteoporosis are a loss of height, a curvature of the upper spine ("dowager's hump"), and a rib cage tilted downward.

As osteoporosis is difficult to treat once the condition occurs, all women should take care to maintain an adequate intake of calcium and exercise. Sufficient calcium is vital, as the body's ability to absorb calcium decreases with age. Unfortunately, most women in the U.S. consume less than half of the calcium they need. The American Society of Bone and Mineral Research recommends that women consume 800-1,000 milligrams a day before menopause, and 1300-1400 milligrams a day after menopause. (One cup of low fat milk, one cup of low fat yogurt and a half cup of cooked turnip greens supply about 960 milligrams of calcium together.)

Milk and dairy products are the best sources of calcium. For those who cannot digest dairy products, sardines, turnip greens, broccoli, salmon, oysters and tofu are good choices. Women who want to take calcium supplements should consult their doctor first, and avoid bone meal and dolomite supplements, which contain lead. Vitamin D is also necessary for calcium absorption. Milk is often fortified with this vitamin, and 15 minutes to one hour in mid-day sunshine will also provide one's daily requirement of vitamin D.

Calcium and phosphorus should be balanced in the diet, which can be difficult to do because so many common foods contain much more phosphorus than calcium—most people consume two to three times as much phosphorus as calcium. Too much phosphorus can hinder calcium absorption. Foods with a good ratio of calcium to phosphorus include cheese, milk, yogurt, broccoli, sardines, corn tortillas, turnip and collard greens. Foods with a higher level of phosphorus to calcium include eggs, frankfurters, lentils, green peas, and lima beans.

Women who smoke, drink alcohol or caffeinated beverages, or use a lot of salt will have higher requirements for calcium.

Regular exercise stimulates new bone formation. Walking, bicycling, hiking and rowing are excellent exercises which place moderate stress on the spine and long bones (arms and legs).

Arthritis

Every 33 seconds, someone gets arthritis in the U.S. Ninety-seven percent of all people over age 60 have some form of arthritis. Arthritis, which actually includes several diseases varying in severity, is the number one crippling disease in the U.S. Much of the crippling caused by arthritis could have been eliminated or reduced if victims had sought early treatment. The average person waits four years after experiencing the first symptoms before seeking medical care.

Prevention:

Daily exercise is probably the most important preventive measure you can take against arthritis. A mere fifteen minutes of steady exercise a day—walking, biking, or swimming, for example—can help keep your bones, ligaments and cartilage strong.

Any extra pounds you are carrying can strain weight-bearing joints and make them more prone to developing arthritis. Try to maintain proper posture and wear supportive shoes. Women should avoid high heels, which distort posture. If you are confined to bed for any length of time, perform slow stretching exercises to keep connective tissue supple.

Treating Arthritis

See a doctor as soon as you feel any pain, tenderness or swelling in one or more joints, any persistent stiffness or tingling sensations in your hands or feet. Therapy may be as simple as aspirin and a regular exercise program, but don't try to treat yourself without seeing a doctor first.

Diabetes

Of the ten million Americans with diabetes, only half of them even know they have the disease. The majority of diabetics develop the disease in mid-life, and are able to control the disease with diet and exercise. One million suffer from the more severe juvenile diabetes, which does require insulin injections. Obesity, illness and pregnancy can all precipitate diabetes.

What increases your risk of developing diabetes?

- A family history of the disease;
- Being overweight, especially if you are over 45;
- Non-whites are 20 percent more likely to develop diabetes than whites;
- Women are 50 percent more likely to get diabetes than men;
- Low-income people are three times more likely than middle- or high-income people to develop the disease.
- With each decade in life, and every 20 percent excess amount of weight, one's chance of getting diabetes doubles.

In diabetes, the body does not metabolize blood sugar properly. Diabetics are more prone to hardening of the arteries, kidney disease and blindness than non-diabetics. Many diabetics, even those with the more severe juvenile diabetes, are able to control their disease so that they suffer only minor complications.

Symptoms of Diabetes

- frequent urination;
- excessive thirst;
- itching skin;
- fatigue;
- blurred vision;
- slow healing of cuts and bruises;
- weight loss despite increased appetite;
- problems with sexual potency.

See your doctor if you have these symptoms. Blood sugar level can often be brought to normal levels through weight loss and diet modification.

Index

139